The Effective Primary Classroom

The Management and Organisation of Teaching and Learning

David Clegg and Shirley Billington

Published in association with the Roehampton Institute

David Fulton Publishers Ltd
2 Barbon Close, London WC1N 3JX

First published in Great Britain by
David Fulton Publishers 1994

British Library Cataloguing in Publication Data

A catalogue record for this book is available from the British Library

ISBN 1-85346-271-3

Typeset by RP Typesetters Ltd., Unit 13, 21 Wren Street, London WC1X 0HF.

Printed in Great Britain by BPC Books & Journals, Exeter.

Contents

Acknowledgements

Many of the ideas within this book are the result of working with headteachers and teachers of Dorset schools too numerous to mention by name. We are very grateful to all of them.

We would also like to thank our typists Chris Oram and June Pinder who have shown enormous forbearance whilst putting this book together.

Finally, we are both grateful for the support of our families, John, Jessica, Kate, Rosie, Harry and Amy.

Introduction

The aim of this book is to bring together a number of aspects about teaching and learning in the primary school. It is intended to be helpful to student teachers and teachers who are concerned to develop and extend their own practice.

The book is primarily a practical one, but where necessary some theoretical issues are touched upon to provide a context for some of the practical ideas. Some parts of the book serve as a rudimentary introduction to aspects of education on which there is already a considerable body of work. Chapter 1 about theory and practice, and in particular the sections which look at learning theories, are there to provide some general background information and to underpin some of the ideas, suggestions and comments on practice. Any reader who wishes to explore these areas in more depth can select from a considerable body of work.

Over the past 15 years, researchers have built up a sizeable body of evidence about what actually happens in primary classrooms. Some of the evidence makes interesting, but not always comfortable, reading. The book brings together elements of the major research programmes over the past years and attempts to make some connection between the various findings. Perhaps the most remarkable feature of the research is the degree of similarity about the findings. We have drawn extensively on this work and it provides the basis of many of our views about classroom practice. We believe it is important that teachers are knowledgeable about this body of research since it is beginning to make an impact upon those who may not be so kindly disposed to what may have hitherto been regarded as the comfortable child-centred world of the primary school.

The last three chapters are firmly rooted in schools and classrooms. Curriculum planning has implications for schools as institutions as well as for individual teachers. What the book offers is a model of planning which will ensure that whole school planning supports and complements a teacher's own curriculum provision. One aspect of teaching and learning which has grown in significance in the past five years is assessment. The book looks at the various aspects of assessment, but focuses particularly on how a teacher can begin to manage assessment in the classroom, use and record the information generated and report to those who need the information. The last chapter of the book takes a close look at organising and managing the classroom.

At the end of each chapter there are a series of 'starting points' which may serve as an introduction to further consideration of the issues raised within the chapter.

The ways in which our young children are educated have changed dramatically during this century. Particular people and events have influenced the organisation of schools and classrooms and the management of the curriculum. Some of the influences run deep, so deep that they have become accepted as unquestionable characteristics of primary practice, rather than being features open to scrutiny and question. It is important that teachers do not cling on to the notion of 'good practice' as an uncontestable and indisputable set of rules for teaching and learning. Good practice, if we are genuine about education, should always be the subject of debate, dispute and contest. It is our belief that the people most able to develop practice are teachers themselves, working with colleagues reflecting upon their own work, and that of their pupils. What we have tried to offer is a framework in which some of that reflection can occur.

CHAPTER 1

Theory and Practice

This chapter provides some important background for other issues raised within the book. In the first section we explore the relationship between theory and practice and try to illustrate some of the complexities within the relationship. We argue that the current political tendency to debunk the role of theory in education is a fundamentally dishonest position which does not withstand scrutiny. The second section of the chapter gives a brief rundown of some of the major psychological influences upon education, focusing particularly on the work of social constructivists, who have placed emphasis on the social nature of learning. In the final section we suggest a way in which teachers can begin to develop their work through reflecting upon their own experience along with that of others, thereby developing a new understanding about their practice.

The Need for a Theory

It was the late socialist historian E. P. Thompson who wrote an essay entitled *The Poverty of Theory* in which he argued against a particular theory of history by demonstrating the theory's inability to 'handle' experience. E. P. Thompson was not anti-theoretical, but he was, as an historian who had enormous integrity, anxious to explore the relationship between ideas and action.

This relationship between ideas and action, or theory and experience, is a central one to education, but anyone who tries to stand firmly with one foot in theory and another in practice will soon realise that the ground is constantly shifting. Not only are theories changing, as we will show, but the relationship between theory and practice is more problematical than it might at first appear.

At the time of writing it is not difficult to identify some perceptions of the uneasy relationship between educational theory and practice. A Prime Minister's[1] speech in which educational theories of the 1960s are cited as the root cause of the perceived fall in education standards,

[1] John Major, Conservative Party Conference 1993.

and the recent proposals on Initial Teacher Training (ITT) which significantly reduce the status of educational theory, are both instances which indicate the current suspicion of theory. Politicians, of course, only point the finger of blame at theories with which they do not agree.

The implication in these instances is that there is a very clear distinction between theory and practice and there is, in fact, a pejorative view of theory, which is that it gets in the way and is unhelpful to practice. There is, therefore, an implicit assumption that effective practice has no basis in theory.

It would be easy for student teachers, and indeed teachers in general, to fall into the trap of this polarisation of a debate about theory and practice. What is currently seen to be on offer is a choice between practice based upon a liberal, child-centred theory of education and practice which takes refuge in what is claimed to be good common sense. The fact that one side of this choice can be referred to as 'common sense' merely indicates the current hegemony enjoyed by a particular 'theory'. What is actually the case is that whether it is articulated or not, all teaching approaches are underpinned by a 'theory'. An approach to teaching in which children sit in rows of desks being told endless facts, is just as much a product of learning theory as one in which children are constantly being urged to discover things for themselves.

This is not to say that all classroom practice must, or should, be dictated entirely by theory, since experience and contingency will have a significant impact upon what happens on a day to day basis. However, without a theoretical framework – a set of beliefs about how children might learn – it is difficult to see how teachers can begin to have a purpose and direction to their work over a period of time. Classroom practice that is not underpinned by a theory about pupil learning has many potential pitfalls, the most dangerous being that it makes teachers vulnerable to fashions and bandwagons and the theories of those in authority over them.

Working with teachers, as advisers and inspectors, we have been particularly conscious that many teachers have a clear perception of our expectations about classroom practice. Many teachers assume we want to see a particular layout and a particular style of organisation. In their efforts to conform to these expectations, they sometimes adopt strategies and techniques with which they are not comfortable, and are merely for our benefit rather than for that of the children.

Our own impressions were confirmed by Alexander (1992) when evaluating the Leeds Primary Needs Programme. In Leeds many teachers rearranged their classrooms, and adapted their classroom management, in response to in-service courses which focused upon classroom layout and the management of various pupil groupings. Teachers adopted ideas and changed their practice, not through discussing how children learn and refining their own understanding, but because there was an assumed view of what 'good practice' (a term to which we will return later) looked like. As Alexander (1992) says:

> If the practice is introduced from a sense of obligation rather than conviction, the adverse effects on children are likely to be even greater.

Unless classroom teachers have a view of how children learn, they will always remain susceptible to the siren voices of either politicians or inspectors. Put in very simple terms, we believe that the way a teacher organises his or her classroom, how the children are managed and grouped, how the teacher spends his or her time, and the nature of the learning activities, should reflect that teacher's views of how children will learn most effectively. Ideally, schools will try to reach a consensus about children's learning and reflect at least a degree of consistency between classes and across year groups, but that is, as they say, another story.

It is perhaps relevant at this point to consider a more pragmatic reason for grounding classroom practice upon some theory, which is connected to the increasing need for schools and teachers to be accountable. Teachers are accountable to various groups including headteachers, governors and colleagues, but also to parents and children. It is perhaps worth considering the last two since they are the constituents who are most likely to ask of a teacher 'Why is my child doing that?' or 'Why do I have to do this?' We believe that both these questions are entirely legitimate and should be answered in straightforward and sensible ways, which demonstrate that thought and planning underpin the activities being pursued. If teachers need a starting point to develop their own theory of learning they could perhaps begin by asking themselves the question 'Why am I teaching in this way?'

So far, we have suggested that teachers will gain confidence by developing a sense of purpose in their practice. This confidence will manifest itself in their ability to resist adopting practices without a sense of conviction and will enable them to give a coherent account of classroom activities to parents and children. If classroom practice is not based upon well thought out ideas about how children learn, then it is not difficult to see how mechanistic, atomised and uncoordinated much of classroom experience would be for both teacher and child.

Having argued in favour of all teachers having a theoretical framework upon which their teaching is grounded, it seems to us that there is an equally important responsibility upon teachers to continually reflect upon and refine their own practice. How children learn most effectively in classrooms should be the subject of professional debate which should not be stifled by any fixed notion of 'good practice', a term which itself tends to reflect a particular theory of learning.

Having established the importance of basing activity on theory, it is important to maintain a sense of perspective. It would be impractical and insensitive to suggest that each activity, each decision, every action should be according to a theory. Life in classrooms is hectic, children's needs vary from day to day and teachers are people with lives outside school which brings its own range of demands and problems. The very nature of the job means that everyday life in a classroom will be governed by routine and by contingency. Teachers get very little time to think and consider when trying to cope with many different and often simultaneous demands. It is understandable that teachers often feel unable to see the wood for the trees, since their lives are spent in a myriad of social interactions.

Having a 'grand plan' for the classroom, and indeed the children, will, however, provide support and guidance to teachers when they consider the more perennial concerns of teaching. These concerns are those aspects of teaching which should inform and support the daily interaction. These aspects include long and medium term curriculum planning, how children's progress is to be assessed, how the room is laid out and organised, the range of learning opportunities to which all pupils should be entitled and the ways in which children should be managed. These are some of the perennial concerns which cannot be adequately answered without a broad framework to inform practice. Having argued for the need for a theory which informs practice, other parts of this book will focus upon some of those constant aspects of teaching and learning referred to above.

Influences on Practice

Child development theories, and the work of a number of educational psychologists, have had a marked impact on the theories of learning which have underpinned various forms of classroom practice.

In the first half of this century, behavioural psychologists, such as Pavlov and Skinner, had an important influence on the ways in which children were taught. There was a perception of children as needing to be told facts in order to increase their knowledge, on the importance of rote learning to absorb information, and on regular periods of practice to reinforce skills and understanding. Hence the largely didactic role of the teacher, and the prevalent formal arrangement of classrooms in which the teacher was a dominant controlling figure and children were passive recipients – or not – of facts. This emphasis on the passing down of knowledge from teacher to pupil results in this being referred to as the transmission model of learning.

The recognition at a later stage that children differ considerably in their rates of learning, as well as there being differences in their experiences, levels of conceptual understanding and degree of confidence and motivation, has highlighted a number of difficulties with this transmission model. The adult must understand what the child knows and can do in order to move learning forward, and the child needs to be committed and involved in the task if learning is to actually take place.

The influence of Piaget changed many educators' perceptions of routes to learning. Piaget saw children's intellectual development as being clearly staged, in which thought developed through active interaction with the environment. The adoption of Piaget's theories resulted in some schools and teachers placing heavy emphasis on the provision of a stimulating learning environment, in which children could explore, investigate and develop their conceptual understanding.

Piaget's analysis of the stages of intellectual development emerged from a series of experiments intended to explore the development of logical thought. He placed emphasis on the importance of practical activity as a precursor to internalised thought and subsequently to more sophisticated mental constructions in which a child attempts to make sense of, and theorise from, his experiences of the world. This process, in moving from concrete operation to abstract thinking, placed a clear emphasis on the importance of play in young children's learning. It is now widely accepted that this stress on play, and the need for a child to experience a series of practical operations, may have resulted in an underestimation of the role of language, and of the need for support from others in promoting children's learning. However, Piaget's major contribution to developing understanding of children's learning was to raise awareness of the fundamental importance of firsthand experience as a basis for understanding. This established a clear role for play as the vehicle for enabling exploration, investigation and representation, and this has been endorsed as an essential strategy in providing opportunities for learning in the primary classroom.

Piaget argued that children's thinking was qualitatively different from that of adults, and that their capacity to understand depended on the child's stage of development. His argument about the relationship between what could be seen, heard and understood had direct implications for teaching. The emphasis upon the need for 'readiness' and the undesirability of teaching children certain things until they had reached a particular stage, underpinned much of the work on children's development which formed the theoretical basis of teacher training in the late 60's and 70's.

Consequently the teacher's responsibility was seen to be primarily concerned with providing appropriate materials and contexts for extending children's experiences, and organising opportunities for the exploration of objects and tasks which would promote their understanding. Indeed, it was suggested that not only were attempts to show or explain things to children before they were mentally 'ready' inappropriate to fostering understanding, but that such forced teaching could confuse and frustrate children and lead to delay in development.

Research in recent years has resulted in a re-evaluation of Piaget's views that understanding depends on developmental stage. Margaret Donaldson (1978) reworked some of Piaget's experiments, and demonstrated that children's apparent failure to carry out certain tasks was due to a lack of understanding of what was required of them. Her experiments, which changed the context of certain tasks and placed them in situations to which the child could relate previous experience, showed the importance of a task making sense to a child if the task is to be achieved successfully. She also highlighted the importance of the use of appropriate language by the adult in enabling a child's understanding.

The work of Donaldson, and of other researchers (for example, Gelman 1969), has demonstrated unequivocally that children can understand abstract problems at an earlier stage than Piaget claimed if they can make connections with the tasks set. If pupils can make sense of a task through familiarity with the context and through the use of appropriate language, then even very young children are able to demonstrate a remarkable level of understanding and ability to reason. Despite this, the notion of 'readiness' has stayed with teachers and manifests itself in many forms. Hence the reference to 'pre-reading' and 'pre-number' tasks in teachers' planning and the occasional description of children as being 'still at the play stage'.

Whilst the general importance of Piaget's work in terms of under-standing children's intellectual development should not be under-estimated, the translation of his theories into classroom practice has had two lasting effects.

Firstly, it has emphasised aspects of the teacher's role as a facili-tator of experiences, provider of materials and creator of a stimulating environment at the expense of the importance of the teacher in directly influencing children's learning. Secondly, there is still a legacy of an underestimation of children's capacity for learning, resulting in some instances in low expectations of children's ability to achieve.

The importance of action and problem-solving in the learning process has continued to form the basis of subsequent work which has influenced classroom practice. A number of researchers have demonstrated that concrete experience is essential in developing child-ren's understanding and in moving them towards abstract thinking. The key point here is that concrete experience is not sufficient as the sole basis for learning.

Bruner, Vygotsky and Wood have highlighted two other areas which appear to be significant in enabling successful learning. These are the importance of the role of a supportive adult, and the crucial nature of language in developing understanding. Although the researchers lay different emphasis on these essential elements of learning, all three have theories to offer which are of importance to a class teacher.

Bruner's 'constructivist' theory assumes the addition or transform-ation of knowledge or information to the existing base of reference. Put another way, the context in which learning takes place is critical in enabling children's development of understanding. Bruner was also very clear that the adult has a crucial role to play in promoting learning and in providing support (often referred to as 'scaffolding') to enable a child to make progress in a particular area. So a child who cannot solve a problem or develop abstract understanding unaided may well be able to do so with support from an adult.

Clearly there would be difficulties for a class teacher in whole-heartedly adopting a constructivist theory and attempting to apply it to working with 30 individuals. Nevertheless, the importance of the adult in enabling the successful construction of understanding has fundamental implications for the way teachers operate in a classroom.

Vygotsky's work created further insight into the processes by which children learn, of which two have particular relevance to work in the classroom. Firstly, the importance of speech for intellectual, in contrast to social, purposes as a prerequisite for thought. Vygotsky argued that young children found it helpful to talk themselves through an activity, particularly to enable them to tackle any difficulties they encountered. Egocentric speech, or a self-directed running commentary, serves as a planning and evaluative tool for children, enabling them to reflect upon and adapt their actions. This process of talking through becomes internalised, developing into inner speech and thought. The point here is that children may be capable of carrying out quite sophisticated mental operations, far exceeding their ability to explain verbally or to record their understanding. The power of talk in developing understanding, and in supporting learning, has only recently been recognised in many classrooms, but the importance of speech in developing higher mental processes is critical. If children are to be expected to plan, organise, review, evaluate and memorise, language is crucial in terms of structuring the processes.

The second key element of Vygotsky's (1962) work is the emphasis on the role of a more knowledgeable 'other person'. He writes of the 'zone of proximal development', which is the gap between what a child is able to do alone and what the child can achieve with the support of someone more skilled or knowledgeable, and can then continue unaided. Within this theory, there is a focus on the importance of a social context for learning. In other words, learning can be promoted and supported through interaction with others, where children can act as peer tutors. So one task of the teacher is to promote learning as a social activity, and to construct an environment which enables 'cooperatively achieved success' as Vygotsky put it. It is very clear that children can play an important role in supporting and enabling learning for each other. The more skilled or knowledgeable person need not be a teacher or other adult since children can, to put it very simply, learn from each other. The recognition of this, and the creation of a climate which promotes opportunities for pupils to use each other's skills and expertise in incidental and informal ways, as well as a more structured situation, needs careful consideration and some explicit development by the teacher.

In a sense, the work of recent researchers such as Wood has brought together the theories of Bruner and Vygotsky in developing a social constructivist view of learning. That is that children are social beings who construct their understanding through interactions in a variety of situations. Within each situation, the learner needs a degree of control over the learning processes in order to construct further understanding. The adult plays a crucial role in supporting the learning process, enabling the child to make sense and move to the next step or zone of development.

So where does this leave the class teacher? Clearly there are limitations in relying on research, particularly that which is theory-based, in that such work is usually quite narrowly focused. There is no possibility that a teacher can successfully implement one specific theory of learning and meet the diverse needs of a large number of children. Indeed we would argue against a teacher trying to do that. The contribution of theory is primarily in terms of the insights which it can provide into possible routes of learning.

What research can enable us to do is to be clear that there are certain conditions to be created if learning is likely to be promoted in the classroom. There are also implications for the role of the adult in creating those conditions and in acting as an agent for learning.

Reflective Teaching

In the first section of this chapter we discussed how important it was that all teachers have a theory which underpinned their classroom practice. This exhortation is in some respects founded on the false idea that theory and practice are two distinct strands within education. As we have said, this myth is perpetuated and indeed promulgated by those in authority who condemn theorists and researchers and claim allegiance to 'good common sense' (whatever that is) as the basis for educational practice.

There is a great deal of literature about the relationship between educational theory and educational practice but it is not the function of this book to reiterate what has been said elsewhere. However, it remains a continuing area of argument and debate and it is important that those who would classify themselves as practitioners are at least aware of some of the emerging consensus views about this particular issue.

Fundamentally, it is increasingly understood that theory and practice are not separate functions because any educational theory must concern itself with educational practice. In a similar way, educational research must address itself ultimately to practical issues. Indeed, by definition education is a practical activity. Issues tackled by educational researchers, such as classroom organisation, the effectiveness of different teaching styles, or the nature of a teacher's role must result in some practical advice, as Carr and Kemmis (1986) point out:

> ...the testing ground for educational research is not its theoretical sophistication or its ability to conform to criteria derived from the

social sciences, but rather its capacity to resolve educational problems and improve educational practice.

The conclusion to be drawn from this is that if theory and practice are not separate, if they are part and parcel of the same enterprise, then all practice must be set within a theoretical framework. Any teacher when challenged about his or her practice will begin to articulate either explicitly or implicitly a set of values and beliefs.

> Since educational practitioners must already have some understanding of what they are doing and an elaborate, if not explicit, set of beliefs about why their practices make sense, they must already possess some 'theory' that serves to explain and direct their conduct. (Carr and Kemmis 1986)

If all practice occurs within a theoretical framework, then we may ask the question 'what is the problem?' If, as we suggested in the first section, all teachers should have a theory which guides their practice and if, as we have just conceded, all practice is in reality guided by some theory, one could suppose that the debate is over. However, any teacher will know that there is always a gap between theory and practice, and this is what creates the dilemma. We can illustrate this by example. A teacher who believes in a formal approach to education will organise learning accordingly. However, if it could be shown that some children did not respond to this approach and were learning very little, this would create an educational problem, which would demonstrate a gap between the theory and the practice. It would be a similar situation if children in a 'progressive' classroom were obviously underachieving. It is the educational problem, the gap between theory and practice, which is the real subject for research, or reflection.

It is important to understand that what we are discussing is not the gap between a researcher's theory and teacher's practice, we are talking about the gap between a teacher's theory and the same teacher's practice because ultimately it is the teacher's theory which will guide any potential solution. As Carr and Kemmis (1986) put it:

> ...the only legitimate task for any educational research to pursue is to develop theories of educational practice that are rooted in the concrete educational experiences and situations of practitioners and that attempt to confront and resolve the educational problems to which these experiences and situations give rise.

From this it is not difficult to begin to appreciate and understand the role of the teacher as both a practitioner and as a researcher. It is this understanding which guides much of the professional development of teachers, in the sense that they are increasingly encouraged to reflect critically upon their practice, and are given the necessary skills and knowledge to enable them to do so. By these means practice can be changed and developed through theory which enables teachers to understand and consider their experiences in a different way.

This discussion serves us well as an introduction to the idea of reflective teaching since it highlights the interaction implicit within the relationship between theory and practice. In reflective teaching, the relationship is more dynamic and more complex than a simple model which would suggest 'this is my theory therefore this is my practice'. An element within the theory of reflective teaching is that teachers must develop the skills and knowledge to enable them to view their practice from a variety of perspectives. This is at the heart of what we mean by being a reflective teacher. It is worth re-emphasising the point which was made in the earlier section, that without this element of reflection, without a rationale for developing practice, teachers are prey to those outside the profession who would wish to dictate or at the very least guide practice in particular ways. If this reflective dimension is present teachers are empowered. They are empowered by their knowledge and understanding and fortified by the confidence they provide:

> Reflective practice in its developed forms requires consideration of ends as well as means. It offers the prospect of giving teaching back to teachers as guardians of a critical and liberal tradition. (Golby 1993)

At this point we can begin to consider in more detail the nature of reflective teaching. Perhaps we should just think about the teacher's role in this. The following extract is adapted from writing by W. G. Perry *Discoveries of the Obvious,* which is quoted by Michael Bassey (1986).

> My fifth discovery was that I am not a watcher of the world, but an actor in it. I have to make decisions and some of them have to be made now. I cannot say 'Stop the world and let me get off for a bit, I want to think some more before I decide.' Given so many differences of opinion among reasonable people, I realise that I can never be sure I am making the 'right' decisions. Yet because I am an actor in the world, I must decide. I must choose what I believe in and own the consequences and never know what lay down the roads I did not take.

Clearly, teachers are actors in the world.

There are many occasions when all teachers are aware of how limited is their impact upon children's learning. This simply reflects life in the classroom, which is often hectic, rushed and relies upon quick decision and some learned patterns of behaviour. Teachers' workloads are increasing alarmingly. Surveys have shown many teachers regularly working between 50 to 60 hours each week in planning, preparing, assessing and recording pupil work. Under these circumstances it is not surprising to hear teachers pleading that they do not have enough time. The constant compromises teachers are forced to make when confronted with a class of 30 or more children are not difficult to understand. To focus attention on one pupil, or a particular group, is to neglect others; to explore one curriculum area in depth may mean some superficial learning in another area. Given this rather pessimistic scenario, it is important to stress that reflective teaching is not just 'something else I have to think about'. Reflective teaching should not be part of the 'problem' but it could be part of the solution in that it provides some guidance about how to begin to manage, organise and develop classroom practice by reflecting upon and confronting some of the everyday dilemmas. It is not a panacea, it will not solve all problems, as anyone who has spent time in a classroom will confirm. The task is never finished or complete. There are always new issues and concerns to be addressed. Reflective teaching may provide both the knowledge and understanding needed to address the issues, and perhaps the stimulation and enthusiasm we all need to tackle some of those dilemmas we encounter.

The ideas around which reflective teaching are based are not new. Dewey in 1933 was pointing to the potential benefits of action based upon reflection rather than habit or routine. It is because the action or practice results from some reflection that it has the potential to change and develop. There are particular characteristics and qualities which feature in reflective teaching and which have been summarised by various writers. The qualities and characteristics are those which would emphasise a professional approach to teaching, but an approach which is concerned with ends as well as means. In this sense, reflective teaching has a broad, social and moral dimension since it is not solely confined to a technical debate about teaching skills. The characteristics therefore are discussed using terms such as 'open-mindedness, responsibility, wholeheartedness, keen observation and reasoned analysis' (Zeichner and Liston 1987). As we can see, it is a complex intertwining of skills and attitudes. Pollard and Tann (1987) summarise the characteristics as follows:

1. Reflective teaching implies an active concern with aims and consequences, as well as both means and technical efficiency.
2. Reflective teaching combines enquiry and implementation skills with attitudes of open-mindedness, responsibility and wholeheartedness.
3. Reflective teaching is applied in a cyclical or spiralling process in which teachers continually monitor, evaluate and revise their own practice.
4. Reflective teaching is based on teacher judgement, informed partly by self-reflection and partly by insights from educational disciplines.

Put in cruder terms, reflective teaching has been described as 'thinking on your feet', with the accent on the thinking! It is also quite fundamentally concerned with teachers learning through experience.

It is this idea of learning through experience which underpins reflective teaching as a cycle or spiral of activity, since learning theories which emphasise the value of experience (for example those of Dewey and Piaget) do so within a cyclical context. This cycle of activity can be expressed in different ways, but essentially the pattern is the same. Experiential learning theory suggests four stages of learning (Figure 1.1).

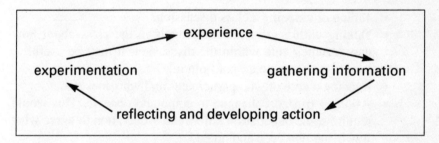

Figure 1.1 – Four stages of experiential learning

Within this cycle reflective teachers will need to draw upon a range of skills, and consider problems within a context of other knowledge and understanding. For Dewey, the learning begins with the experience which may present itself as problematic. The reflective teacher then steps back from the problem and begins to ask himself or herself some searching questions:

What was the precise nature of the problem?
What was my intention?

What did I actually do?

What in fact happened?

What may emerge is a discrepancy between intention and outcome. Identifying the problem is therefore an important aspect of the process. Solving the problem will require reflection, and this may mean referring to colleagues, applying acquired knowledge or skills, and then reformulating action. It may be helpful if we use an example to illustrate the cycle.

The experience. The introduction of the National Curriculum has raised the awareness of the importance of speaking and listening. This may in turn give rise to some anxiety on the part of a teacher about the majority of pupils within a class appearing reluctant (or unable?) to participate in a class discussion. The teacher may decide to observe this situation more closely.

Gathering information. In this context, observing refers to gathering a range of information which would inform the reflection. This means the teacher must begin to investigate the precise nature of class discussions, and must collect some data. There are clearly different ways of doing this but the following would be helpful:

- Taping or videoing a class discussion.
- Talking with a group or individuals in the class about how they see their role within the discussion. It may be useful to target children who do not 'join in'.
- Keeping a note of who participates and who does not.
- Asking a trusted colleague to come and observe. This would require some negotiation before the observation to agree what was being observed and noted.

Gathering the information above will not solve the problem. The teacher will need to reflect upon what has been discovered and will need some knowledge about how to evaluate and react to the information. This could necessitate the teacher engaging in some modest research into the nature of classroom talk and how it can have an impact on learning. For example, in this instance an awareness of the work of the National Oracy Project would be helpful.

Reflecting and developing action. Through this process of information gathering and research the teacher would be able to look at the information in a particular way. He or she would be able to analyse the structure of the discussion in terms of the nature of teacher questions, the implicit pupil response time, the appropriateness of the language, the style of teacher response to answers or the dominance of the teacher. In other words, a teacher needs the skills to gather the information, and then the knowledge and understanding about how to respond to and reflect upon the information. In this part of the process the practitioner is reformulating his or her thoughts about classroom discussions and is also beginning to develop some ideas to try out in the near future.

Experimentation. In this final part of the process the teacher puts some new ideas into action. This may involve changing the nature of the discussion from whole class to smaller groups, it may involve thinking more carefully about the wording of questions and the nature of the response. In any event, it will also involve further monitoring and evaluation on the teacher's part and so the cycle begins again.

Finally in this section it is worth dwelling for a few moments on the potential benefits of working closely with a colleague. In the example above it was suggested at one stage that teachers could help each other through observation and discussion. Working with others within this reflective framework not only means sharing the load, but aiding the process of reflection through discussion. This mutual arrangement could have various characteristics. It could be a relationship between two colleagues who share values and beliefs about education, or it could be a relationship between colleagues one of whom is more experienced as a practitioner, but is similarly committed to the idea of reflective teaching. In the latter case there could be an element of coaching or facilitating on the part of the experienced practitioner which may provide some very valuable support.

What this chapter has tried to show is the dynamic relationship between theory and practice and how this can enhance the development of effective teaching and learning. We have emphasised that practice expresses implicitly a particular set of beliefs and understandings, but we would suggest that the most effective teaching is developed by a process of reflection upon those beliefs and understandings and the subsequent practice. Part of the reflective process is concerned with developing and using the knowledge and skills which facilitate reflection so that teachers are able to be both practitioners

and researchers. The following chapters attempt to explore aspects of
the framework within which a teacher can consider his or her own
work in the classroom.

Starting Points

The Need for a Theory
- Do you have a clear overall view of how children's learning can be
  supported and developed?
- How does your practice reflect that theory of learning?

Influences on Practice
- Have you thought through the role of the teacher in creating 'appropriate conditions for learning'?
- Are you clear about the implications of the various theories and
  research which are helpful in thinking about your role as a teacher?

Reflective Teaching
- Is your practice set within a framework of theory?
- How is your practice influenced or amended in the light of
  experience?

CHAPTER 2
Children Learning and Teachers Teaching

This chapter is about primary school classrooms. It is perhaps useful to remind ourselves that any research, thoughts, theories or ideas about education must, ultimately, address what happens in classrooms. The chapter is divided into three sections. The first explores some ideas about the social nature of classrooms which it is easy to overlook in discussion about psychological theories of learning. Psychologists concerned with researching how children learn provided teachers with significant and valuable insights, but usually overlooked, and in fact were not concerned with, the dimension of the classroom. Formulating and testing hypotheses about how children learn will contribute to the development of appropriate pedagogy, but we must always remember that this book is not about children learning in general but about children learning in classrooms. Classrooms introduce a 'social' dimension insofar as a classroom is made up of a group of people operating within certain constraints bound up with the nature of relationships, societal expectations and the location of power. Any discussion therefore about teaching and learning must explore the social nature of classrooms.

The second section will develop the view of classrooms further. It will explore recent research into classrooms and demonstrate what we are beginning to understand about what may make some classrooms more effective than others. The section will draw upon some of the major research projects over the past decade which have looked closely at classroom practice and try to bring together some of the findings which may demonstrate some characteristics of effective classrooms. The final section of the chapter will focus in detail upon some of those issues, and examine some fundamental concerns about effective teaching strategies.

The social context of teaching and learning

The physical context for learning after the age of five is, for most children, the classroom. How this is organised and managed will have an impact upon learning, and that is the subject of a later chapter. The social context of learning, rather than the classroom and the class, is a group of children, sometimes of a similar age, sometimes not, but all different, together with a teacher and possibly the periodic presence of other adults. It is the dynamics of the relationships with the class which have an impact upon learning. Teaching and learning do not occur within a vacuum. They are processes which are subjected to stresses and strains created both from within and without the class.

The impact on learning of the dynamics of classroom life is not divorced from learning theory. As we have already discussed, the work of Vygotsky and others has emphasised the importance of learning as a social activity. We have noted that one of the prerequisites of successful learning is interaction with others, whether a parent, teacher or peer. This emphasis on interaction allows teachers to look again at classroom practice and evaluate activity within a framework which gives central importance to the social nature of learning. In this sense the classroom is able to become the focus of learning not simply from expediency, but from design. In other words, a dimension of effective learning is that children need to be with other children. Towards the end of this chapter we look in some detail at how children can support each other's learning, but it is sufficient at this point to remember that the classroom is where learning theory and group interaction coincide, or in other words where psychology and sociology meet.

There are three elements to the social dimension of the classroom. There is the pressure of societal expectation, the pupils themselves and how they behave and react, and the teacher. We will consider each of these in turn.

Society has an ambivalent attitude to education. There is often an incongruity between people's collective experiences, or perceptions, and the individual experience. Opinion polls will generally confirm that people think that educational standards are falling, whilst research has also demonstrated that over 80% of parents are satisfied with their own children's primary school (Hughes et al 1990). It is difficult to explain these findings without going into areas of social psychology, but it does demonstrate the difficulties facing schools and the pressures on teachers.

It is not within the scope of this book to rehearse the argument about whether standards of education have fallen or risen, but what would seem to be clear is that expectations of education have risen significantly. We need look no further than the National Curriculum documents themselves to see what is expected of primary education. It is a strange paradox that whilst research demonstrates that it is increasingly unrealistic to expect teachers to have the range of subject knowledge and expertise to teach pupils aged 10 and 11 years the full scope of the National Curriculum, someone clearly expects pupils to learn it! Society's expectations of school however are not simply confined to the academic. Teachers are often regarded (to varying degrees) as the moral guardians of young children and indeed society. Schools are seen as places where children should be 'trained' as well as educated, and an element in the training is the necessity of some conformity. This is a large subject which raises very important issues, not least of which is conformity to what? However the point we are making is that there is an expectation on the part of society that schools, and therefore teachers, have some responsibility to introduce children to the values which underpin our society. This expectation is made quite explicit when a lack of discipline in schools is cited as one factor in causing juvenile crime. Any discussions about values is always problematical, but the Secretary of State has made it very clear that schools should not be 'value-free zones' and indeed schools will be judged on their ability to promote pupils' spiritual, moral, social and cultural development. In many teachers' eyes, schools have become easy targets and a convenient scapegoat. Perhaps this pressure should not be overestimated, although it has had an impact on teacher morale. Schools should encourage the communities they serve to develop some understanding of education through direct experience against which they can test public and political rhetoric. Society's ambivalence to education is an important issue for schools. In the new climate of accountability, it is important that schools do not become defensive and insular. The way forward is for schools to encourage and seek the involvement and support of their local communities and ensure that all parents are aware of what the school is trying to achieve through its curriculum.

Further pressure is currently being exerted through the emphasis on 'back to basics', and again exactly what this means is open to some dispute, but the use of the term 'back' would certainly imply a degree of nostalgia and an effort to reverse current trends and return to a past era. The interpretation in schools may well be that primary education should be centrally concerned with teaching children basic skills – enabling them to develop a range of learning competences including literacy and numeracy. No-one would argue much with that, but the call for a 'back to basics' implies that at some point in the recent history of primary education a decision was taken to encourage schools not to attend to the basic skills, despite the overwhelming evidence of Her Majesty's Inspectors that primary schools have consistently devoted a disproportionate amount of teaching time to English and mathematics. The real pressure here is for primary schools to successfully teach the 'basics' within a curriculum that is broad and balanced.

Whatever the theories and practice teachers bring to bear upon the classroom, they operate within a particular political climate which can introduce pressures and constraints that affect what happens in classrooms. This political climate of operation will also be part of the ideological background, which is unavoidable but not always comfortable. There will always be signs of stress and conflict when schools work on the edge of what represents the climate of operation. One example of an issue which created a wide fault line was 'real books'. This issue was represented only by the two extreme viewpoints of the progressive versus traditional debate. The fact that virtually no schools relied totally upon an unstructured approach to the teaching of reading got quite lost in the ensuing debate. Any school which incorporated the concept of 'real books' as part of its teaching strategy, however, found itself being accused of almost wilful neglect of the teaching of reading.

It is within the climate of operation that pupils and teachers encounter each other. Both bring their own expectations and anxieties into the classroom, and it is to the 'people' we must now turn. Many schools work very hard to ensure that children are introduced to school in a supportive and positive way. Children and their parents are often invited into school on formal occasions prior to the official starting day where efforts are made to familiarise children with the geography and atmosphere of the school. Some schools make a point of visiting each child at home in an attempt to begin to forge the important home–school partnership. These efforts are vital in ensuring a smooth transition from home to school, but they cannot alter the fact that home and school are very different environments. How pupils adapt to the environment and begin to make sense of it, research suggests, has some impact upon their academic achievement (Jackson 1987). It is likely that for many children school will be unlike any other environment they have known. They will have to become familiar with new rules and new regulations, and they will develop a wide range of new social relationships. The transition from the home environment to school has been described by Cashdan (1980) as the move from the à la carte menu to the table d'hote. Quite suddenly a child's world may be closed down. Choices will not be available, and attention will not be provided to anything like the same degree. How children adapt and respond to this situation, what Margaret Jackson (1987) refers to as their social competence, is linked to their academic achievement.

Once pupils are settled into routines and their relationships are established, they begin to behave in certain ways. Children will often make subconscious choices about how they will behave, and teachers have perceptions of children which correspond to identifiable patterns of pupil behaviour. Andrew Pollard (1985) identifies groups of children with common characteristics and classifies them into goodies, jokers and gangs. These labels are self-explanatory and will strike a familiar chord with many experienced teachers, but, for our purposes, the important point to understand is what is happening when children adopt the behaviour patterns which correspond to one of the above classifications. They are clearly expressing elements of their personality, but also, and more fundamentally, they are adopting a mode of behaviour which they see as protecting their 'self'. They are behaving in a way which is designed to get them through the day with their self-esteem intact – in the eyes of the teacher, of their peers, or of both. It is the dilemma posed by 'who do I please, my friends or my teacher?' which is often a real one for children, and, of course, they make a variety of choices. In other words, some children prefer to protect their self-esteem by demonstrating their ability to break rules, not conform and appear apathetic to school. In these instances they may be maintaining their 'self' in the eyes of their peers but not their teachers. Other pupils will make different choices, they will conform and maintain their self-esteem by pleasing a teacher, or indeed by simply keeping out of trouble. The problem for some children is therefore how to interact successfully with both pupils and teachers. Pollard also makes the important point that what induces this determination to protect the 'self' is the evaluative nature of classrooms. If judgements are constantly being made about a child's work, behaviour, or attitudes, then clearly that is a potential threat to their self-esteem, and therefore pupil behaviour is often going to be defensive against this threat. Put another way, if a child sees that by completing a task about which he or she is unsure there is a risk of a rebuke for getting it wrong, or of being compared with other children and being seen to have done less well, then it is quite understandable that there may be reluctance to complete the task!

It is through this kind of action that children learn to deal with what may be a threatening environment. Coming to terms with this, coping with it, is in fact the children learning to 'make sense' of the world.

How children choose to make sense of their circumstances will depend on various factors. All children need status, so that they can develop their own self-esteem. Children need to like themselves, before they are able to like others and form successful relationships. Factors which affect how children see school will include gender, social class, race and the degree of success they achieve, and this will also have an impact on how they will seek status. Some will seek status by conforming to school expectations, others will find solace in gaining peer approval through being seen as non-conformist and unafraid of stepping outside the boundaries. There are important practical lessons to be drawn from this which concern the way pupils are treated and regarded, but before moving on to that we need to consider how the teacher sees the classroom and how they respond to their own set of social circumstances.

There are some similarities between the concerns of teachers and those of the pupils they teach. Teachers are faced with some clear dilemmas about their position and their role, and are, like the children, concerned to protect their 'self'. On the one hand they represent authority, but at the same time they want pupils to be involved in their own learning. Although in authority and being the centre of power, the teacher is lonely, and can readily appreciate the potential for chaos or conflict inherent in confronting perhaps 30 children. Teachers are also subject to the expectations of society in a way that children are not, and feel the weight of expectations that they will maintain control and keep a sense of order. This determination to control is therefore firmly embedded in many teachers, as it not only meets the expectations of the world at large, but it is also through control that the teacher protects him or herself. If things get out of control, teachers are vulnerable to their colleagues, children and the outside world. Pollard (1985) suggests that this urge to keep control (not, we hasten to add, in any malicious or unpleasant way) was the main reason why the revolution in primary education following the Plowden Report never actually took place. Quite simply, most teachers were reluctant to give sufficient authority or indeed responsibility to the children.

A teacher's reality is firmly rooted in experience. Most teachers share a pragmatism born from working with a constant awareness of a certain vulnerability, and they therefore place great emphasis upon 'what works'. At *worst* this can produce unhelpful cynicism on the part of teachers who are being asked to do a job within a climate of rising expectations and a lowering of resources. For those teachers, what works may be defined simply in terms of what keeps children busy, and enables control to be maintained. At *best* it produces a healthy scepticism which matches innovation against experience alongside a professional determination to do the job as effectively as possible. What works for these teachers may be defined through that process of reflection we discussed earlier, but will focus upon children learning rather than just their busyness.

Perhaps this is an overly pessimistic view of the primary classroom. Certainly the thought in most teachers' minds at the start of each day is not 'I must keep control', and for the most part they are not governed by the fear of classroom chaos and anarchy. At the same time, however, it would be disingenuous to dismiss the pressure that teachers do feel as a result of legislation which has raised parental expectation and ensured that teachers are accountable for their work in a very public way.

This is a view of the classroom which perhaps moves us away from the direct concerns of learning theory, but it is important that we remember that the classroom is not an idyllic environment untouched by society. It is the place where formal education by and large occurs and therefore the dynamics which are at work in all classrooms is an important dimension in any discussion about teachers teaching and young children learning.

Reconciling the position of teachers and children is not too difficult. It is the responsibility of the teacher to ensure that the various anxieties are overcome since it is they who have the power of making quite fundamental choices. The way the teacher chooses to act largely dictates the classroom climate.

These are very real and important choices which are embedded in everyday classroom activity, but which nevertheless should be the result of long term goals. These choices will require thought about:

- how to respond to children's work;
- how to achieve and maintain a calm working atmosphere;
- what are to be the acceptable norms of relationships;
- what should be the balance between sanctions and rewards.

Perhaps more fundamental to this is the question about how these decisions will be made, and what part, if any, will pupils play?

Andrew Pollard (1985) urges that teachers adopt what he refers to as 'a social policy for the classroom'. The idea of having a policy implies a long term view about establishing a classroom climate which will support and promote children's learning. It implies for teachers that they should have a concern for the means of education as well as the ends. In classrooms which have good climates for learning, the actual creation of the climate is purposeful and an integral part of the learning process. Making the above choices will necessitate the implicit adoption of a social policy which provides a framework to support everyday transactions.

An effective social policy will be sensitive to the issues we have already discussed. There will be an understanding of the need for all children to protect and develop their own self-image and this will be promoted through clear action. It should include the following considerations:

- the efforts of all children should be recognised and acknowledged;
- grouping children must be done in a manner which protects their self-image;
- classroom rules and sanctions should be the result of some discussion or at the very least some explanation.

There is more to say about classroom climate, but that will be looked at in more detail in the next section.

What we know about effective classrooms

Within the debate about primary education, it is sometimes overlooked that we know a great deal about what actually happens in classrooms. This knowledge has been gained in two distinct ways. Firstly, there has developed over the past 15 years a body of academic research which is firmly grounded in classroom observations and has provided us with some clear insights into teachers teaching and young children learning. Secondly, there has been a steady stream of reports published by Her Majesty's Inspectorate (HMI) based upon their many visits to primary classrooms which have provided further information. What is quite remarkable about both bodies of evidence is the similarity of the findings. Over the past several years what has emerged from a detailed analysis of primary classrooms is a series of pictures which bear many similarities. Each new piece of research evidence has largely confirmed previous findings rather than producing a series of conflicting messages.

There is at this point the need for a word of caution. It would be understandable for anyone to ask why, if we know so much about effective classrooms, we do not just put all those features or findings into place and thereby make all our classrooms more effective? If only life was so simple and straightforward! There are several difficulties with that approach. Research, whilst being valuable, is limited. When classrooms are observed they are different environments to when they are unobserved. The very presence of an observer changes the nature of the classroom and potentially alters the way teachers and children behave. No classroom observations are entirely objective because observers will bring their own prejudices and values to bear upon their interpretation of what they see and hear. It is also notoriously dangerous to transfer findings unthinkingly from individual classrooms, or single schools, to other classrooms and schools because, as any teacher knows, all classrooms are different. Since classrooms consist of people engaging in a variety of relationships, there is enormous scope for unpredictability in terms of behaviour. What may be a highly successful teaching strategy in one classroom in a particular school may be an unmitigated disaster in another. That's because the people are different, they have different backgrounds, different beliefs and different histories.

Whatever research tells us about 'effective classrooms', if we as teachers are to benefit from it, we must adapt the findings to suit our own particular situations. If research tells us that learning is most effective when the teacher interacts with the whole class rather than individuals, it would be foolish to simply plan each day around a series of whole class lessons in the hope of being more effective. How a teacher responds to such a finding will depend on many things, but one will be the specific circumstances of the class. A teacher in a small rural primary school teaching three or four year groups in one class will respond quite differently from a teacher teaching a single age group class in an urban school.

Some of the findings from research projects may make uncomfortable reading; indeed, some findings will contrast sharply with what some teachers would claim to be 'good primary practice'. We believe that this body of work should not be ignored, and further suggest that we should pay particular attention to those findings which do seem to question some long held notions of good practice. We believe that 'good primary practice' as a fixed, unquestioned concept has diminished aspects of the legitimate debate about primary classrooms, and we have no intention in this book of replacing one view of good practice with another. We believe that it is for teachers to think about and adapt their practice, taking into account their experience and their knowledge. What the following summary of findings will provide is a research framework within which we suggest that all teachers and all schools should seek to define a view of good practice which is appropriate to their own circumstances. We also think that part of that process is an understanding and welcoming of the fact that, even within individual classrooms and schools, effective practice is not fixed, but is constantly being adapted and refined. This picture of how classroom practice develops should sit comfortably with the earlier view of the reflective practitioner.

What follows is a general summary of the findings of research projects undertaken in the last 15 years. Within the summaries it will be evident that there are particular aspects of classroom teaching which are regularly shown to be important. Towards the end of the chapter we will focus upon those classroom issues which do seem to have a direct bearing on the learning process, and refer in more specific terms to some aspects of the research projects.

Neville Bennett was the first researcher to investigate classrooms in the period after the publication of the Plowden Report. His initial work focused upon teachers' behaviour, and he drew the conclusion that the style of teaching made an impact on children's performance. This study, published in 1976 as *Teaching Styles and Pupil Progress,* was subsequently seriously questioned, but it created a climate which encouraged similar, but more carefully mounted projects. Bennett himself began to revisit some of the issues which had emerged in the earlier study, in particular focusing upon the pupils' activity. Further work that he published in 1984 suggested that two important factors in the effectiveness or otherwise of the learning experience were, first, the 'match' between the difficulty of the task and the ability of the child and, second, the amount of time the child spent on the task.

The question of 'match' became (and remains) a crucial issue. It was a research finding which backed up the views of HMI who consistently reported that children were often asked to complete activities which were ill-fitted to their abilities. This was usually linked to low expectations of pupils by teachers as tasks were deemed to be too easy and 'lacking in challenge'. The issue of match also raises two other important issues. Firstly, if matching the activity to the child's ability is so important, then it reinforces the need for careful assessment of the child's ability. Secondly, it also throws some light upon the sheer enormity of the teachers' task in providing suitable tasks for 30 children who may have considerable differences in ability. Any research which focuses upon pupil activity will highlight the distinction between children doing something and children learning. This is an important issue which will be explored in a later section of this chapter. Work by Wragg, Bennett and Carré (1989) carried out since the introduction of the National Curriculum has also suggested that a teacher's subject knowledge may have an impact on pupil performance. This is hardly surprising since, as we have already noted, there is a very significant body of knowledge required to teach 10 subjects up to the end of Key Stage 2.

In 1980, a team of researchers led by Maurice Galton based at Leicester University published a major research project based upon systematic classroom observations. The ORACLE[2] project, as it was called, continued to publish further findings throughout the 1980s. Like the work of Bennett, it has had a lasting impact upon the way classrooms are viewed. Galton's team began to classify teachers into various types defined by their classroom behaviour and what effect these types had on pupil attainment. What emerged was that no single 'teacher type' was significantly more successful than all others, although some types were generally more successful than others. This led the team to try to identify those classroom strategies or modes of operating which were shared by the most successful types of teacher. The result was a list of strategies which other researchers have only been able to confirm rather than challenge. Those teachers who were most successful shared the following attributes:

- all ensured that routine activities were performed smoothly;
- all engaged in more than the average number of interactions with pupils;
- all engaged in high level questioning with pupils and provided children with regular constructive critical feedback;
- all encouraged children to work things out for themselves.

What this list emphasises is the importance of providing opportunities for high quality teacher–pupil interaction. We will look more closely at some issues surrounding the use of talk and the quality of teacher–pupil interaction in a later section, as well as picking up the issues touched on above. Before moving on from the ORACLE study however, it is important that we look at some of the other findings by Galton, which also support the work of Pollard (1985) and the social context of learning. Galton gathered evidence to illustrate the bargain which is struck between children and teachers. Pupils will cooperate and get on as long as the teacher provides work which is non-threatening and safe in the sense that it does not threaten to expose their ignorance. This has a knock-on effect. If children perform and behave best when doing low-level tasks, and if they feel threatened and anxious and therefore perform less successfully when confronted with activities which have a degree of ambiguity within them and

[2]ORACLE – Observational Research and Classroom Learning Evaluation.

make new demands upon their abilities, then this will influence the level of teacher expectation. Children will also protect themselves by slowing down their work rate. For instance, if pupils are working through a maths book and are quite aware that when the current page is completed they will turn over and begin the next page which contains problems which are more difficult, they will be in no rush to complete the current page. Unless the teacher is aware and acts upon this, the pace of learning could be quite slow.

The list of attributes shared by those various types of teachers in the ORACLE study provides a useful comparison with the work of Peter Mortimore and his team (1988) at the now defunct Inner London Education Authority (ILEA). This important project followed a group of junior aged children through 50 schools, and was concerned to identify characteristics of schools which were more effective than others. The project used a variety of research methods, including questionnaires to teachers about their practice followed by classroom observations. One interesting finding was that teachers often behaved differently from the way they said they behaved. For instance, most teachers when interviewed reported that they spent most of their time interacting with the whole class, whereas observation of these same teachers showed that most of their time was spent in interacting with individuals.

What the project also established was that some schools were more effective than others in terms of pupil progress, and some of the factors which seemed to promote pupil progress were (not surprisingly) found in individual classrooms. The research concluded that the most effective classrooms often had the following features:

- Teachers were largely responsible for ordering the activities throughout the day, although pupils had some responsibility for structuring their work within individual sessions.
- Sessions only covered one curriculum area at a time.
- There were frequent interactions between the teacher and the whole class.
- Good use was made by the teacher of high-order questions and statements.
- Appropriate, well-matched and challenging activities were provided.
- The atmosphere of the classroom was positive with an emphasis on praise and encouragement.

It is not difficult to discern the similarities within this list and those proposed by the ORACLE team. What is emphasised is the nature and quality of teacher–pupil interaction and the apparent inability of frequent contact between the teacher and children on an individual basis to consistently generate the high quality interaction possible through group or class discussions. *School Matters* (Mortimore 1988) also reinforces the quality of the activity as a crucial element in developing learning.

Perhaps more surprising are the findings concerning the structure of the day and the emphasis upon one curriculum area. A message that would appear to emerge is that junior age pupils should be offered a careful balance of choice and direction: too much choice and they will not receive a balanced and broad curriculum, too little and they become too dependent. Choice, therefore, should be structured within a clear framework, but that framework must allow for the acquisition and development of skills which will promote independence. Focusing upon a single curriculum area in one session will present a significant challenge to what has become a traditional way of thinking about the primary curriculum. This result could be interpreted as a direct attack upon the topic or project-based approach, or upon the classroom organisation associated with the integrated day whereby children move between a series of activities which each have a distinct curriculum focus. Curriculum organisation and management will be discussed in some detail in a following chapter, but it may be relevant at this point to simply remind ourselves that if a class is studying only one curriculum area it does not mean that every child is doing the same thing, it only means that all children are engaged with the same subject. If they are all focusing upon the same subject then it provides more opportunity for the teacher to engage with the whole class about specific teaching points and problems.

A similar study undertaken in London infant schools by a team working with Barbara Tizard (1988) concluded that children's attainment in basic skills was closely associated with the amount of exposure they had to a curriculum which focused upon these skills. They found that some teachers did not introduce young children to certain aspects of learning on the basis that it was 'too difficult' for children of their age. Other teachers, who worked with children of similar ages and backgrounds, exposed children to a wider curriculum and therefore implicitly demonstrated higher expectations and promoted greater progress in children's learning. We can begin to see further similarities here with previous studies, highlighting the importance of teaching expectation and the range and quality of learning activities.

The final, and most recent, piece of large scale research which we will look at is an evaluation of a project which was mounted by the Leeds Education Authority. The team of evaluators was led by Professor Robin Alexander from Leeds University. Before looking at the conclusions it may be helpful to provide some background information to the project. The Leeds Primary Needs Project began in 1985 and involved the injection of a significant amount of finance from both central and local governments. Between 1985-89 the Leeds Council invested almost 14 million in the programme. The final evaluation report was published in 1991, the so called 'Alexander Report', and provoked a nationwide controversy about the nature of primary school teaching. A book containing the report, but expanding some of the ideas and setting the conclusions within a clear context, was published in 1992.

The Alexander Report, although focusing upon one Local Education Authority, has significance for all primary schools. The conclusions are certainly challenging and some of the ideas provide fertile ground for our continuing debate. Perhaps, though, it is important to bear in mind that it is one of a series of studies based upon classroom observation and is therefore within the same tradition of educational research as that conducted by Bennett, Galton, Mortimore and Tizard. What the conclusions do, in a very powerful manner, is reinforce most of the conclusions from previous research. Alexander provides a picture of classroom life which will now be very familiar and which includes the following:

- the difficulty of managing activities concerned with different curriculum areas occurring at the same time;
- the importance of the appropriateness of the learning activity;
- the ineffective use of teacher time when the predominant interactions are with individuals;
- the importance of the quality of the interactions and the low level of questions and classroom discussions;
- the reluctance of teachers to provide critical feedback to pupils about their work or contributions;
- the comparative absence of collaborative group work.

The Alexander Report occurred at a time when primary education was under scrutiny and it made perhaps more impact than previous similar studies. It was used to fuel a more vigorous debate.

What has been developed over the past 15 years is a significant body of evidence about what factors are important when considering the effectiveness of primary classrooms. Much of this evidence was brought to bear upon the discussion paper, issued by the then Department of Education and Science (DES), called *Curriculum Organisation and Classroom Practice in Primary Schools*. This discussion paper was put together to encourage a debate about some of the central concerns of classroom practice which we have touched upon in this section. The paper provided a framework for the discussion by drawing upon the evidence from the various projects we have outlined as well as the routine observations undertaken by Her Majesty's Inspectors. The framework made reference to aspects of classroom practice such as:

- teachers being confident in the subject they are teaching;
- teachers having appropriate expectations;
- the importance of teachers planning their work;
- efficient use of teacher time;
- promoting an appropriate classroom climate;
- the importance of assessment in 'matching' work to children's abilities;
- the use of a wide range of teaching strategies;
- the effective use of talk.

A further follow-up report was issued to all schools in 1993 from the newly formed Office for Standards in Education (Ofsted). This revisited much of the ground, but provided a list of factors which HMI considers to be 'associated with better classroom practice' (Figure 2.1). The list has a familiar ring and its pedigree has been well established.

The most significant feature of the various research projects are the similarities of the conclusions, but we must guard against assuming that what is being indicated is a new orthodoxy, a new version of good practice. We must resist this temptation and, as Alexander remarks, treat the idea of 'good practice' as problematical rather than fixed.

The research projects we have considered provide teachers with a framework to guide their discussions about practice, rather than providing answers. There are some interesting and challenging ideas within the research, but there are also things that will come as no surprise to many experienced teachers. For example, it is not surprising that the quality and nature of learning activities are important in developing successful learning, any more than the suggestion that purposeful interactions between teacher and children are desirable in promoting understanding. More challenging, however, is the

Organisational strategies
- Carefully planned and appropriate groupings of pupils for tasks.
- A mixture of individual, group and whole-class teaching.
- A manageable number of teaching groups and learning activities, usually four or fewer, provided in the classroom at any one time.
- Carefully planned use of the teacher's time for giving instructions, teaching the whole class, individuals and groups, and moving between activities to instruct, question, explain and assess.
- Planned use of the pupils' time including the setting of realistic deadlines for the completion of work.
- Clearly established classroom routines and systems.

Teaching techniques
- The use of good oral instructions to set the scene and to explain tasks to the whole class or to a group.
- Opportunities provided for pupils to raise questions about tasks or activities and for the teacher to listen to the pupils.
- Skilful questioning to encourage the children to think and use knowledge already acquired.
- The observation of pupils' work and of pupils at work to help with assessment; careful and regular monitoring of pupil progress.
- Teacher interaction and purposeful intervention in pupils' work.
- Appropriate use of teacher demonstration.
- The use of good work by pupils as a model for others.
- Teaching targeted to specific individuals or groups.
- Appropriate use of praise and encouragement.
- Feedback to pupils during lessons.
- Continuous assessment as an aid to the learning process.
- Criteria for assessing work made explicit to the children.

Teachers' knowledge
- Sound understanding of the subject matter to be taught.
- Sound knowledge of the pupils' current levels of achievement and the levels to which they should be progressing.
- Close familiarity with National Curriculum programmes of study and statements of attainment.

Figure 2.1 – Factors associated with better classroom practice (Ofsted, 1993)

consistent evidence of low expectations on the part of teachers and the subsequent dampening down of pupil achievement. The most challenging aspect of the evidence may rest in the suggestion that teachers' rhetoric about children and learning is not apparent within their practice. It is an uncomfortable situation when primary school teachers, with the best intentions, aim for every child to fulfil their potential, and yet so often underestimate that potential. It is equally disconcerting for primary school teachers who have a concern for the individual child to be confronted with evidence which suggests that the more they interact with some individuals, the less other individuals make progress. It is also uncomfortable, given that there is never enough time, to consider evidence that teachers do not always use their own time in the most effective ways.

These ideas, however, should be the subject of debate. The research does not reveal a new way of doing things but provides some insight through which the reflective teacher can begin to consider his or her own practice. The final section of this chapter, and indeed the remaining chapters, begin to explore the major themes which this brief review of recent research has highlighted.

Teaching strategies

Pupil Activity

When asked to consider the range of activities in which pupils become engaged in a classroom, an initial response from a teacher may be to categorise these activities in terms of the subjects which they represent. This is a logical and in many ways perfectly understandable route to take, given the concerns of teachers to cope with National Curriculum requirements, but there are other methods of looking at the way pupils function in the classroom and we would suggest that it is important to consider pupil activity in broader terms.

The variety of research carried out over the past 20 years contains some critical messages for teachers eager to increase the effectiveness of their work, and we have already explored some of these in the section on effective classrooms. In returning to some of the same research we will now focus particularly on issues related to pupils' activities in the classrooms and ways in which learning can be promoted, or indeed hindered, by the nature of the tasks in which they become engaged.

Neville Bennett's early work focused very much on various teaching styles and their apparent effect on children's performances in English and mathematics. Although the validity of the study was queried in terms of its design and analysis, it did raise some fundamental questions which were pursued further. These related to pupils' experiences in terms of time 'on task' and the match of various tasks with pupils' learning needs. Bennett identified these as key elements in the 'opportunity to learn' paradigm. So the nature of pupils' engagement with a task is critical in examining the relationship of teaching to learning. There are several dimensions within that pupil–task relationship which the reflective teacher will wish to explore further.

Bennett (1987) gave some indication that time on task is not sufficient as the sole condition for learning:

> There is little to be gained from high pupil involvement on tasks that are either not comprehensible or worthwhile.

In other words, pupils can spend a great deal of time on tasks that achieve little in terms of pupil learning.

This was reinforced by the work of Tizard et al (1988) which looked closely at the use of time in a number of infant schools in London. Apart from the study identifying how little time was actually available for classroom-based learning activities (46%), attention was paid to evidence of children's time on task. The children observed were engaged in their tasks for 61% of the available time. However, many of the tasks were fairly low level and repetitive in nature. Given this, there might be a degree of surprise in such a high level of application, but the evidence would appear to confirm Galton's view of children slowing their work rate to match teacher expectation, and Pollard's description of the unspoken contract between teacher and child. Children's desire to please the teacher and to conform to implicit expectations that they get on, keep busy and complete given tasks would appear to carry many of them a long way through some dull situations!

Alexander's study of work in Leeds primary schools showed similar figures for children's time on task (Table 2.1). The important information in the context which we are discussing is in the first column, the time spent working, 59% being the average for all curriculum areas, but with some marked differences in terms of pupil application in various activities.

The information provided relates to a pupil's activities across subjects and is particularly significant when thinking about task design in the classroom. Teachers ask children to demonstrate their understanding in various ways, but the most common is to ask for it to be written (in a variety of forms). It is worth reflecting on the limitations this places on many pupils whose capacity to understand, reason, solve problems and apply skills will be greater than their capacity to record any of this in written form.

	Working	Routine	Awaiting attention	Distracted	Not observed
Writing	52	13	8	28	<1
Apparatus	65	12	6	17	<1
Reading	57	12	6	24	<1
Listening/looking	68	6	10	15	1
Drawing/painting	55	14	5	25	1
Collaboration	67	11	6	15	<1
Movement	54	15	14	17	<1
Talking to teacher	71	11	6	10	2
Construction	70	7	3	20	0
Talking to class	100	0	0	0	0
All activities	59	11	8	21	1

Table 2.1 – Task-related behaviour in different generic activities (percentage of pupil time) reproduced from Policy and Practice in Primary Education – Robin Alexander (1992)

Children spent a significantly higher proportion of their time working when they undertook tasks which involved other people. Talking to the teacher or to other children, collaborating, listening and/or looking and construction activities had a high level of engagement. Writing, drawing or painting and reading had a low level of application to task, and the highest levels of distraction. It is worth noting that these activities were generally carried out in isolation, again highlighting the importance of the social context for effective learning.

The quality and appropriateness of tasks set has been a constant theme of HMI reports, which have regularly raised concerns about poor match. The work of Bennett and Desforges demonstrated that even in classrooms of teachers cited as 'good', only 40% of tasks were judged as matching pupils' capabilities.

Given the expectation that a teacher should manage the learning of a large number of children with a wide range of needs, the whole area of match of task creates almost impossible demands. The need to be aware of it as a critical dimension of appropriate provision may have been masked by some of the other concerns about managing learning which we have already cited. The implicit assumption that busy classrooms are automatically places of learning has created a self-perpetuating myth which has influenced various aspects of a teacher's practice.

Hence tasks may often be set which will cover many curriculum areas simultaneously and will create an impression of a great deal going on. In this situation, pupils may appear to be focused on their individual tasks, there may appear to be a good level of concentration and application, and the teacher is likely to be extremely busy instructing and supporting pupils in groups, or as individuals. A superficial view of this type of classroom situation might convey an impression of a very hardworking, even overstretched teacher, as he or she may be, and pupils getting on with their work in a bright, busy classroom. All too often in these instances, assessments of pupil learning by teachers, or visitors to the classroom, may be based on the amount of activity rather than the appropriateness or quality of the tasks set.

This is confirmed by our own visits to classrooms where teachers have a tendency to become almost apologetic in a situation where a tightly directed whole class lesson, such as handwriting practice, is taking place. As with pupils having certain perceptions of teacher expectations, it appears that many teachers have implicit views of what inspectors want to see! Again an assumption is made that busyness in the form of lots of activities, group work and so on will be viewed as indicators of an effective learning situation.

Bennett's work on classroom tasks suggested that 75% of those set in English demanded practice of pupils' existing skills or knowledge. Whilst practice and reinforcement are necessary aspects of learning, this figure suggests a disproportionate allocation of time to these aspects in contrast to that available for the application and development of skills. This clearly raises further issues related to planning for a balance of opportunities for learning development.

The study also highlighted the particular difficulties inherent in meeting the needs of both high and low attainers in a class. There was a similar pattern of task design for both groups, though the actual content might differ. Whilst high attainers were consistently underestimated, the abilities of low attainers were frequently overestimated. Interviews with teachers in the course of that study were frequently of the view that if children appeared busy, appropriate demands were being made of them. This again confirms the problem of the 'busyness' syndrome in masking what is actually happening in terms of learning opportunity in the classroom.

Observation of teachers in the classroom established that teachers were quick to recognise where a task was too difficult, but rarely saw where it was too easy. In the former situation, signs of difficulty are of course likely to be fairly obvious, such as pupils asking for frequent assistance, being unable to complete a task or becoming very distractible or even disruptive. Indicators in the latter case, where a task is too easy, are likely to be more obscure. Pupils may complete a task quickly or, as we have discussed earlier, may slow their work rate to match teacher expectation or risk being given more of the same to do! They may also have a range of strategies to enable them to appear occupied, and the nature of their compliance with a task can often mask the lack of challenge within it. The study also confirmed that in terms of assessing pupils' learning, the focus of a teacher was frequently on the end product of a task, rather than looking closely at the process which had led to that. The message here is clearly that in order to assess the appropriateness of the match of task to pupil, it is fundamentally important to gain a view of the pupils' engagement with the task in the course of it being undertaken, rather than at the stage of completion.

In order to ensure that children are kept busy, a high proportion of tasks may be set which are scheme or worksheet-based. Given that much of this type of work requires filling in missing words, completing sentences or sums, or, in many cases, colouring pictures, children's activity may be often of an occupational nature. This type of activity will go on in most classrooms from time to time for perfectly valid reasons. What is clear however, is that in many class-rooms a large proportion of time is spent on these types of occupa-tional tasks and that many children are therefore marking time in terms of their learning development.

The challenge then for teachers is to take account of the findings about task design and match, and to examine closely the range of activities available in their classrooms, and the ways in which they are organised. Given the range of information now available on use of time in the classroom, the nature of pupil activity and the match of task to cognitive ability, the teacher is left with the challenge of taking these issues into account whilst planning and managing the work of around 30 children with wide-ranging needs and abilities.

There are some critical factors to be considered in planning appro-priate activities for a class, which will influence the quality of pupils' learning. The question that needs to be at the forefront at any stage of planning is 'what do I want the children to learn?' Only when that is clear can decisions be made on how that learning opportunity can be provided and which activities will best support the planned learning intentions.

In thinking through that initial question 'what do I want the children to learn?', it is important to be clear that 'learning' in this context will take a range of forms. It may indicate the introduction or acquisition of new knowledge or skills. It may also mean practising a process, consolidation of facts, applying information in a new situation, restructuring knowledge, exploring possibilities in an experiment or attempting to solve a problem. Learning does not always mean moving onwards or upwards. It may mean extension, application, practice, experimentation, or repetition. The point is that the last of these – repetition – tends to dominate a great deal of classroom activity unless *learning purpose* is at the forefront of planning and provision.

Given what we know about pupils' engagement in tasks, it is also important to plan for a balance in the range of activities in which pupils are engaged. If learning is promoted and enriched through interaction with others, then planning for that interaction to take place is critical. If application to task is greater in a range of practical activities which promote opportunities to talk and collaborate, ensuring that there are sufficient opportunities for paired, group and whole class work to take place is fundamentally important.

As discussed earlier, match of task to ability is an aspiration rather than an absolute in an effective classroom. 'Match' does not necessitate providing individual programmes for 30 or more children. That would clearly be impossible, and it should not be necessary. What it does mean is teachers asking themselves very critical questions about the way they plan and organise tasks in the classroom, and the programme which is offered to the class. No class of children needs an identical programme of activities. Pupils may engage in the same task, perhaps together or perhaps in a group or individually over a period of time. If the task is providing an appropriate experience for all pupils and if they can achieve differing outcomes, or have access to varying levels of support or range of resources in the course of that task, it may be appropriate for all to undertake it. So one task at differing levels may be perfectly valid.

It may also be possible to provide one task, probably over a lengthy period of time, which will enable all pupils to practise and develop a range of skills in the course of a single activity. For example, if pupils are involved in book-making, they will have opportunity for designing, planning, illustrating, editing, redrafting and presenting. They will need different levels of support or materials in the course of this, but can all engage in a learning process and produce an appropriate outcome.

Task setting in classrooms can, and should, take a variety of dimensions. Teachers can set a context for learning which includes a range of opportunities for pupil activity. Once again the key issue in this is 'balance'. This will include setting short-term tasks that may require assigned work to be completed within a specific timescale, and providing some long-term activities where pupils can make decisions about routes to take, materials to use and the nature of the outcome. Pupils will need opportunities to practise or develop knowledge or skills, and also opportunities to use previously acquired knowledge or skills in a new activity. The provision of opportunities to make investigations, to confront problems, to respond to open questions will engage pupils in tasks which have a degree of challenge.

In creating this context for learning, the importance of the teacher as a model for pupils cannot be overemphasised. The degree of enthusiasm and interest which a teacher brings to the classroom will be reflected in the attitude of pupils to the activities offered. The attitude of the teacher in confronting problems or errors will be transmitted in the ability of pupils to find a route through an area of difficulty.

At the same time, it is important to be aware that effective learning can take place without direct involvement of the teacher. Indeed it must do so or the pace of learning in most classes would be very slow. Making full use of the resources available in the classroom, having a range of self-maintaining tasks, and providing activities such as a 'challenge of the week', will create opportunities for learning outside the planned programme of tasks.

Many teachers organise a range of activities for pupils to undertake outside the time when they are working under teacher direction. The form of these will obviously vary according to the age of the pupils but might include for younger children maths games, making zig-zag books, adding structures to a class model of a street, sharing a 'book of the week' with a friend and so on. Older pupils can be set a maths problem, undertake a science investigation set up in a small area of the classroom, research some specific information on the current topic or develop a display area.

All these type of independent activities can be very useful, but they do require some planning and monitoring by the teacher. Careful explanation of the purpose and nature of the available tasks and some opportunity to draw together what pupils have discovered, or discuss what they have produced, are important in demonstrating the validity of work undertaken independently, alongside that in which the teacher leads or participates directly. In addition, if learning is a social activity then creating a range of situations which will promote pupil discussion, strategies for peer support and shared review and evaluation should be critical elements in creating an effective learning context.

Classroom Talk

No-one spends long in a classroom without beginning to appreciate the amount of talk which occurs within the course of a normal school day. The nature of the talk will be varied. Some will be pupils chatting together, sometimes about their work; at other times about something outside the immediate concerns of the classroom. Some talk will be between the teacher and individual pupils, groups of pupils or perhaps the whole class. Teacher talk will take many forms, and may be instructions, statements, questions or even exclamations. The nature and quality of classroom talk has been the subject of considerable debate following the emergence of learning theories which have emphasised the social nature of learning. This section will look at some of the issues which teachers should consider if they want talk to be effective in developing children's understanding. We will concentrate on what can be called purposeful talk rather than talk which could be referred to as incidental conversation.

Any exploration of the nature and quality of classroom talk generally arrives at two overriding conclusions. First, that in terms of quantity, teachers talk too much and children talk too little. Second, in terms of quality, much of the talk in classrooms is concerned with low level activities such as maintaining routines or monitoring pupil work. This situation persists despite the repeated findings that a high incidence of good quality talk is a consistent feature of effective classrooms. Alexander (1992) found that:

> Classroom talk, despite the conversational liveliness of many classrooms, could be shown on closer examination to be somewhat impoverished and unchallenging, with a general tendency to discourage children from asking their own questions and thinking things out for themselves, and a lack of informative feedback.

Mortimore and his colleagues (1988) make a similar point in a slightly more positive way, and concluded that good communication has a positive effect upon pupil progress:

> There was strong evidence that those teachers who spent greater

amounts of time communicating with pupils about the content of their work had a positive effect upon progress in all cognitive areas....The amount of teacher time devoted to giving pupils feedback about their work also had a positive association with progress in a number of areas.

A further dimension within the verbal interaction in classrooms is time and how it is used. Teacher time is the most valuable resource in the classroom and there are ways and means of creating 'time to teach' rather than it being eaten up by routine administrative matters. However, creating the time is not an end in itself. What is much more important is what a teacher does with the time created. It is at this point that the nature of classroom talk can have a direct impact upon the development of learning.

The issues of quantity and quality of talk are not unconnected, but the aim of any classroom should be to involve all children in high quality talk. This is not to say that teachers should not talk, but that the frequency and nature of their utterances and how these encourage children's talk should be given some consideration. Where talk is used well, teachers use it in a variety of ways which can be classified into:

- questions
- instructions
- critical feedback.

There are of course many other types of talk, but much of it will inevitably be concerned with routines and maintenance of the teaching session. Before looking at each of the above types of talk it is important to reinforce the importance of time. All teachers are faced with a constant dilemma and this dilemma is clearly apparent when we consider talk. The dilemma is that the more time a teacher engages in high quality talk, or any other purposeful activity, with pupils as individuals, the less time each individual pupil is able to engage with the teacher. Because of this constant paradox, one dimension in all our discussions about talk is the most effective use of time. In other words, developing a mode of questioning which develops learning is important but also knowing when to employ the mode with individuals, groups and the whole class is equally critical.

Questions
Teachers use questions a lot. In fact it has been estimated that in an

average professional lifetime a teacher will pose up to one and a half million questions. Other research has found that teachers pose on average about two questions per minute, whereas a class of pupils between them raise about two questions per hour. One study in pre-school playgroups (quoted in Wood 1988) showed that 47% of teacher utterances were questions, in an American High School it was 43%. For the pupils within these studies the figures were 4% and 8%. Again, these quantitative findings are reinforced by the work of Alexander (1992):

> Though questioning was a prominent mode of teacher discourse, the full potential of questioning as a teaching strategy was not always exploited. Thus questions might feature as little more than conversational or rhetorical devices; they might be more token than genuine; they might be predominantly closed; and they might lack cognitive challenge. Moreover, in some classrooms where teachers asked many questions, their pupils were able to ask relatively few, and having done so they might risk having their questions blocked or marginalised. Teachers were clearly conscious of the pressure of time and the need to cover the ground intended. Yet the urge to press on, paradoxically, could lead to questioning becoming not more but less effective and therefore a somewhat inefficient use of the time available.

This paragraph raises issues as well as confirming some impressions. It raises the issue about 'genuine questions' and what that might mean. There are many occasions when teachers ask questions which are not genuine in the sense that they are not asked in a spirit of enquiry – since on many occasions teachers already know the answers – and they are usually only concerned to find and acknowledge that specific answer. Questioning in this mode is often a sort of cloze procedure in which pupils have to guess the word in the teacher's head. Such sessions usually lack any clear purpose, and waste a considerable amount of time.

The notion of closed and open questions is one that has been the subject of some debate. The majority of questions teachers ask are 'closed' in the sense that they are not speculative nor open to a variety of responses. They are closed in the sense that there is a wrong or right answer and to give the wrong answer closes the dialogue. Closed questions are not always inappropriate. If a teacher wishes to assess pupils' knowledge and understanding, asking a series of closed questions can be quite appropriate. For instance, questions such as:

What is the capital city of...?
What happens to water when the temperature drops below freezing?
Who assassinated President Lincoln?

These types of questions are perfectly legitimate if the intention is to assess children's knowledge and understanding. However, if the intention is to encourage children to think, then the questioning should be more open, it should invite speculation, encourage a variety of responses and pose genuine dilemmas. These types of questions can be framed in different ways which can be challenging, exploratory or investigative – questions such as:

Why do you think...?
What would happen if...?
How do you think such and such a person felt...?
Can you think about...?

These questions not only encourage thought, reflection and some analysis but they also invite a dialogue and discussion between either a teacher and pupil, pupil and pupil, or teacher and a class.

Class discussions are still effective ways of promoting understanding but they need careful handling. They are less effective when the teacher dominates and provides all the information, and is stubbornly single-minded about the intended outcome. Conducting a discussion amongst a group of pupils or the whole class is precisely that – conducting. Contributions can be encouraged by questions which engage pupils in dialogue, by setting up oppositions or dilemmas. The teacher's role here is to listen and orchestrate, not to feel obliged to make the biggest contribution. All teachers should strive to achieve a balance between open and closed questions. Too often the balance is weighted in favour of closed questions, while more open questions would encourage more thought and also demonstrate the genuine spirit of enquiry we want to promote.

The pressure of time is also keenly felt when asking questions. This need to cover the ground leads not only to questions being superficial, but also to answers being demanded very quickly. The average response time pupils are given after a question is in the region of one second. If no answer is forthcoming most teachers move on. Experiments to lengthen the time pupils are given to respond to up to three seconds have demonstrated that pupils' responses have increased in qualitative as well as quantitative terms (quoted in Wood 1988). However, the same experiments showed that teachers found it very difficult to wait three seconds for a response. We can only speculate why this should be the case, but it may have something to do with the pressure and need to move on, and the assumption that silence equals ignorance. What we may also speculate upon is that with the current demands of the National Curriculum this situation is unlikely to remedy itself.

Given that teachers find it difficult to give pupils sufficient time to respond, and also given that any questions posed, closed or open, are potential threats to children since they provide an opportunity for them to demonstrate their ignorance, perhaps questions are not the most productive way of encouraging pupils to talk, question and think.

> The more questions the teacher asked, the less children had to say. The pupils were also less likely to elaborate on the topic of talk, ask questions or to talk to each other when teacher questions were frequent. (Wood 1992)

David Wood suggests there are alternatives to questioning which are significantly more productive in eliciting a wider range of, and more animated responses from, children. Children are more likely to respond if the teacher uses other modes of talk, such as that which is speculative, or informative, hypothesising or recounting a personal experience. In this way teacher talk becomes more effective in that it promotes more pupil talk, and is less threatening because it is more conversational.

These alternatives to questioning are useful modes. They often provide insights into children's thoughts and therefore their understanding, which questioning often inhibits. Certainly our own experience would confirm the view that children will more readily engage in conversation when we have used the above strategies in preference to direct questioning. In the course of classroom visits it is still difficult to stop ourselves opening up a dialogue with groups of children by asking 'what are you doing?' Increasingly our experiences suggest that if we really want to engage with children about their activity, a different approach is more productive. Sometimes it is better to say nothing, watch and wait, and often children will initiate the conversation. Another strategy is to simply make a contribution through recounting a personal opinion, experience or offering an idea. The idea of 'joining in' equalises the interaction, whereas questions and answers often reinforce the power relationships within the classroom.

In summary, questions play a big part in classroom dialogue. All teachers need to be clear about the range and type of questions they use and to ask themselves whether questioning is always the most productive way of encouraging children to talk, listen, discuss and generate their own questions.

Instruction
Instruction is an unfashionable word in education. It has connotations of hierarchy, and powerlessness; instructions are passed down and the receivers of instructions by definition have little autonomy. Another powerful metaphor for instruction is the sergeant major on the parade ground, or the coach on the sports field, barking out instructions with aggression apparently designed to motivate. In the world of primary education, where the language is less harsh, learning is spoken of in terms such as discovery, growth, exploration and activity. Instruction does not sit comfortably with received ideas about teaching. It is perhaps time for it to be reinstated in teaching, and for instruction to be recognised as having a significant place within a teacher's repertoire. We are not discussing instruction here in the way it was described earlier. No-one wishes the classroom to resemble the drill hall, and no-one wishes to see children as simply receivers of instructions. Nevertheless, instructing is a powerful way of developing learning. It is concerned directly with providing children with assistance, not only by telling them information, but through pointing things out, reminding them of previous learning, providing insights into the significance of their discourses and helping them to see their learning in a wider context. Instruction can be employed by a teacher at different times, and have different purposes. At the beginning of activities, clear instructions need to be given about the kind of framework within which children will work. The activity will be more successful if children are clear about the purpose, the ways of working, the choices open to them, and the criteria for making any judgements about their achievement. For instance, a simple early writing exercise for very young children is to draw line patterns between parallel lines. Before this activity is undertaken, it could be explained to children that this will help them to develop skills they will need later for writing letters, that they will work on their own, that they may choose which colour to draw the line, and that you will be looking for lines which are continuous and in between the parallel lines. In this sense the instructions would be clear.

Instructions can also occur during a teaching session when pupils are already engaged in an activity. On these occasions teachers are able to provide the kind of instruction which Wood refers to as the 'seemingly simple and trivial things' done to help children:

> Pointing out, reminding, suggesting and praising, all serve to orchestrate and structure the child's activities under the guidance of one more expert. (Wood 1988)

The point made here about structuring the child's activity is an important one. The role of instruction is not to simply assist in the immediate activity, since it has a much more enduring role to play. According to Vygotsky, the external voice of the instructor gradually becomes the internal voice of instruction. Tharpe and Gallimore (1988) put this point well:

> It is important that instructing be acquitted of any bad name, because the instructing voice of the teacher becomes the self-instructing voice of the learner in the transition from apprentice to self-regulated performer. The non-instructing teacher may be denying the learner the most valuable residue of the teaching interaction: that heard, regulating voice, a gradually internalised voice, that then becomes the pupils' self-regulating still small instructor.

Instructing is therefore fulfilling a dual purpose. It is assisting the learner at an immediate level as well as in the longer term. Instructing should not be confused with directing, as it is concerned centrally with assisting and supporting learning. The support or help is not given by telling children the answer or providing them with a solution – although there is nothing wrong with telling children things! It is about helping children to find solutions to problems by asking the right questions, providing some insights and making connections with earlier learning. In this way the nature of the assistance is closely concerned with teaching children to learn.

Critical Feedback

In some respects, the idea of being critical in relation to children's work is another one which does not rest easily upon the shoulders of primary school teachers. It is part of the same unease we have about telling children they are wrong. It is part and parcel of the primary school teacher's concern to raise and maintain the self-esteem of all children through being positive and placing an emphasis on praise rather than disapproval.

We do, however, have to distinguish between criticism which is destructive and that which is constructive. The former will undermine confidence and demotivate, whereas the latter may provide opportunities to develop and build upon what is already learned. Perhaps a more helpful way of thinking about the idea of being critical is not to think only in terms of judgements being made, but to think in terms of importance. If something is critical it also implies it is important, and this further implies that it should be subjected to a reasonable degree of rigour. Certainly there is a good deal of evidence to suggest that rigorous, critical feedback to children about their work does make an impact upon their progress (Mortimore et al 1988, Tharp and Gallimore 1988).

Critical feedback shares some similarities with instructing, in that it has the potential to have a double impact upon pupils. Critical feedback can have an immediate impact upon the work in question. For instance, feedback about a story or a model in progress should render a more successful outcome; feedback on work completed should provide help to improve future outcomes. There is also, however, a more lasting benefit from giving critical feedback since it is demonstrating to children a way of thinking about their work which, if it becomes internalised, provides them with an approach through which they can begin the process of critical reflections for themselves.

If any feedback is to be effective, it should begin by recognising and acknowledging a pupil's achievement. In this way a child's self-esteem is developed, and a degree of trust is built up which allows for a more rigorous appraisal of the work in question. This appraisal should be positive in the sense that it should be made clear to children how the work could be improved rather than simply denigrated or dismissed. It should also have an element of dialogue so that the child is being challenged to think carefully about aspects of the work.

On some occasions, other children in the class might be involved in providing some feedback. This could be a feature of all classes, but it needs developing carefully. Teachers must understand that for some children this will be a very threatening situation, and so the ethos of the classroom has to be built up so that there is an approach to working which is mutually supportive, where mistakes are seen as opportunities to learn rather than as being simply wrong. Having said that, it is our experience that most children enjoy opportunities to see other children's work, and in most cases are eager to praise and acknowledge the achievements of their classmates. Remember, critical feedback is positive and useful!

If children are to be offered effective critical feedback there is another major implication for teachers. No feedback can be effective, and no judgements fair, unless children know the purpose of the activity and the criteria for judging success. There has often been what can only be described as a conspiracy of silence on the part of teachers about telling children the purpose of what they are doing. Edwards and Mercer (1987) pick up this point in their classroom research:

> It appears to be a valued and common practice that teachers will conduct an entire lesson, or series of lessons and never feel it appropriate to tell the pupils why they are doing particular activities, or where it all fits into what they have done and will do next. This appears to be no accidental state of affairs. The avoidance of explicit communication of the goals and contexts of classroom activity is a consequence of teachers' educational ideology – that pupils are essentially individuals in pursuit of a realisation of their own individual potentials, that they are not to be told things, that they should learn things for themselves.

Key elements in any effective curriculum are that it should be relevant and purposeful. If this is to be achieved, if pupils are to see the relevance and purpose of what they are doing, then they must be told why they are doing things. If judgements are to be made, if pupils are to be offered critical feedback, then teachers must refer to the criteria for making the judgement.

It is demonstrably the case that most children, if asked to define the feature of a piece of work which the teacher regards as good, will mention criteria such as appearance, neatness, perhaps spellings and sometimes length. Whilst in no way diminishing these aspects of work, it may well be the case that the teacher may be looking for ideas, particular constructions, or use of words. In other words, there is great potential for misunderstanding through lack of explanation on the part of the teacher and misconceptions on the part of the children.

In summary, critical feedback has been clearly identified as a feature of effective learning. To make it effective it has to be positive, and made meaningful by relating it to purpose and intention. Children should be clear about why they are doing an activity, and what the teacher may be looking for in the outcomes.

Pupil Organisation

All teachers will find themselves working with the whole class, small groups of pupils and individuals at various times for a variety of purposes. There has been a great deal of recent debate and rhetoric about the respective merits of these forms of organisation, with the implied assumption that class teaching represents the formal didactic approach and group work a progressive child-centred style of teaching. Despite this, the fact is that all these strategies for pupil organisation will have a place in an effective classroom.

In making decisions about ways of managing their pupils, teachers have to consider the question of what they are trying to achieve in terms of pupil learning. What is to be taught, and by implication learned, should determine the type of organisation which will be most efficient and effective. Each of the approaches has particular merits but also some drawbacks, and in deciding which to use teachers will need to ask themselves some critical questions:

> What do I want the pupils to learn?
> How can I make best use of my time in teaching this area of the curriculum?
> Do I need to cover this with all of the pupils?
> Will I need to organise this in a number of different ways for different pupils?

Whole class teaching
Whilst whole class teaching may be the usual form of organisation for subjects such as music or at storytime, it is a strategy which is generally used for an introductory session leading to group activities. Whole class teaching can therefore act as a scene setter and be used for the assignment of tasks, but as a teaching strategy it has got considerable potential beyond that. It does create a situation where the teacher is very much the focus of attention, and it is an opportunity to demonstrate a skill or technique, to explain routes through an activity, to initiate a discussion, to highlight successes or difficulties in tasks being undertaken and to lead a shared experience. Managed effectively, whole class teaching can create a shared sense of purpose, and through clear explanations, statements and skilful questioning can lead to a high level of pupil involvement and response.

The difficulty associated with whole class teaching relates to the level at which it is pitched. Inevitably, there is a tendency to aim towards the middle of the ability range, thereby offering little but confusion to children of low ability, and perhaps only a limited degree of challenge and involvement to more able pupils. The skilled teacher will take account of this and aim to provide appropriate information, explanation or questions for children of different ability levels, but it is no easy task. Being clear about the purpose of working with the whole class, and ensuring involvement of individual pupils can, at times, make whole class teaching an effective strategy for advancing pupil learning.

There will be times, too, when drawing the attention of the whole class to some work in progress, or the ways in which a particular group or individuals have tackled a task, will enable the reinforcement of particular teaching points or create an opportunity for further instruction. In this sense, class teaching can be used effectively in the middle of a teaching session or for evaluations at the end.

Individual teaching

There will also be occasions when working with individual pupils is essential in developing their skills and understanding. There is an important distinction here between individual teaching and organising individual tasks. An example of individual tasks would be pupils working through a scheme for mathematics or English at their own pace. This again raises the question explored in the earlier section on pupil activity – is being occupied and busy necessarily synonymous with pupil learning? The situation of pupils working on routine tasks on an individual basis will arise in every classroom for very pragmatic reasons. In any class of average size it would clearly be impossible to ensure that learning was continually moving forward, and there will, of necessity, be some work of an occupational nature. As we discussed earlier, what is important is to ensure that this is not the predominant form of activity.

In contrast, individual teaching is a sustained opportunity for a teacher to instruct, explain or demonstrate at an appropriate level for a pupil. Undoubtedly all pupils would benefit from this situation, but to try to provide it for every child would result in minimal interaction between teacher and pupil, frequent interruptions from other pupils needing support and therefore low gains in pupil understanding. As we discussed in the earlier section on talk, a teacher faces a dilemma in deciding how much time can be spent with individuals, since the more this is done, the less time is actually available for pupil interaction. Again it is important to be clear about the purpose of teaching on an individual basis, which may be quite justifiable at some times for some pupils, and ensuring that this can be managed to allow sustained and challenging teacher–pupil involvement.

Group work

Given, therefore, the impracticalities of individual teaching and the drawbacks associated with whole class teaching, it is not surprising that the predominant form of organisation in classrooms is grouping. This can take a variety of forms, the most common being by friendship, ability, or mixed ability. There is an important distinction to be drawn between group work as a management strategy, which essentially involves pupils sitting together but working on identical or similar tasks on an individual basis, and group work which involves pupils working on a collaborative basis. Both forms of grouping have a place in the classroom, but the purposes of the groups differ, as do the skills required of the pupils involved. Whatever form is used, effective group work demands careful preparation and management on the part of the teacher.

It will also demand a degree of flexibility in organisation. If pupils remain in the same groups for a substantial length of time, they are quick to recognise the rationale which underlies the grouping. Even very young children are remarkably adept at recognising grouping based on ability level, and are able to place themselves and their peers in order according to academic ability, with a good degree of accuracy. However teachers might describe the groups, using a variety of names based on colours, animals and so on, children will still be quick to understand positions in ranking and can begin to label themselves or others. There can be a noticeable effect on pupils' self-image, and indeed on teacher expectations of pupils' potential for achievement, in such situations.

That is not to say that grouping by ability is not a perfectly valid strategy at times. It can be a powerful and effective way of working, provided that the teacher is clear about the reasons for organising the pupils in this way. As with being clear about the learning intention before deciding on the appropriate task to achieve it, the most effective form of grouping to promote learning outcomes also needs to be planned.

The curriculum areas which perhaps lend themselves most readily to grouping regularly by ability are mathematics and some aspects of English. It may also be appropriate to use ability grouping for other subjects at times, particularly for teaching a specific skill or technique or to begin to develop a particular concept. The key point here is that the grouping arrangements for pupils, in all their various forms, need to be considered carefully alongside other elements of planning for pupil learning.

There is considerable evidence, however, (Cohen 1986, Galton and Williamson 1992) that grouping low-attaining pupils together can have severe disadvantages, and the effectiveness of this strategy has been questioned. There tends to be a considerable demand on teacher time to support these groups, difficulty for pupils in understanding and interpreting the tasks set and an inability on the part of those involved to communicate together as part of the process, or to support each other in the course of the task set. The outcomes are often of poor quality. Again that is not to suggest that low-attaining pupils should never work together, but what the teacher needs to guard against is getting locked in to a particular type of grouping which is based on pupils' ability levels in a particular subject, and which becomes the prevalent form of organisation for much of the time. In considering some of the questions we raised in the introduction to this section, a teacher may well decide that the learning needs of a particular group of pupils may be best met if they work together. This might enable efficient use of teacher time and an effective opportunity to cover an area of the curriculum with a small group. A key factor in ensuring success in the activity would seem to be the involvement and support of the teacher through the task, which would need to be planned for in advance of the teaching session.

Grouping by friendship or through pupils' free choice is common for many activities. The advantage of self-selected or social groups is that pupils will have a shared base or some common interests, which are likely to enable them to work well together. They will probably generate a sense of motivation in undertaking a task, and may well be able to work towards a shared outcome. However, if pupils always work with individuals of their choice or with a particular friendship group, they can have quite narrow experiences in terms of their social or cognitive development. The development of tolerance and patience with others, and the opportunity to consider an alternative suggestion or point of view, may not be particular features of a group activity based on friendship. They are, however, important experiences in learning to collaborate successfully in many areas and to work at establishing relationships.

Planning the composition of groups is therefore likely to be necessary from time to time if pupils are to have opportunity to work with an appropriate range of individuals. In planning groupings, teachers will need to be aware of issues related to gender or race and guard against pupils working in groups based on these factors unless there is an appropriate reason for them to do so.

A variety of research has focused on the effect of gender on classroom groups. Where friendship groups are encouraged, pupils will generally work with others of the same sex. Even if mixed sex groups are organised, 80% of conversation is between members of the same sex (Galton et al 1980). There may be occasions, however, when single sex grouping is an effective strategy. It has been suggested, for example, that this will enable the development of particular skills in girls in aspects of technology which are frequently dominated by boys. A teacher's own observation in the classroom may indicate that certain areas of it are dominated or neglected by groups of boys or girls – the role play area for example being one that is frequented more often by girls. In these types of situations, ensuring that all pupils have equal access to the available curriculum opportunities may necessitate some single sex grouping.

There is insufficient evidence to show whether pupils in single sex or mixed groups achieve more, though there are indications that time on task is greater in mixed sex groups. In considering gender as a factor in grouping, teachers will want to consider social as well as academic factors, or may well decide as a matter of principle that working with peers of both sexes is a key developmental experience for children.

For many aspects of the curriculum, mixed ability groups may be appropriate in supporting learning aims and ensuring opportunities for pupils to work in a variety of settings. As discussed earlier, ability groups may be an appropriate form of organisation to enable teaching to be closely aligned to pupil needs, but there is considerable evidence that mixed ability groups can be helpful in meeting a wide range of learning needs.

The work carried out by Bennett and Dunne (1992) and by Webb (1989) suggests very clearly that able children do not necessarily need to work together to achieve optimal outcomes. The most able children perform well no matter what form of grouping is used, and in fact Webb established that if they were together, there was a feeling that cooperation was unnecessary, resulting in a lack of investment in a group activity. Webb also established that the least able children achieved little in a situation where they were grouped together, or they lacked the necessary knowledge, skills or organisational ability to cope with the task. Her work indicates clearly that mixed ability grouping can be effective in meeting needs across the ability range. Where high attainers were spread across groups, there was a good degree of successful group activity, without any apparent loss of attainment for the most able.

Bennett and Dunne suggest that high-attaining children can be challenged by the need to cooperate in a task and to ensure its successful organisation as well as by its cognitive content in a mixed ability group. In their study of 11- to 12-year-olds working in mixed groups, on-task behaviour was of a high level, and instructional talk substantially greater than organisational talk. There was concern, however, for less able children if the group composition was inappropriate. In a group of three, two able children tended to talk together and exclude the less able child. Where the reverse configuration occurred, an able child could successfully support two less able with ideas and explanation, so that all involved had some understanding of and commitment to the task.

A range of research has looked at the issue of group size, with a variety of findings. Most teachers seat pupils in groups of around four to six, probably reflecting their efforts to make best use of the space and furniture available in the classroom. Groups of six, or even more, may be quite appropriate in terms of planning a specific teacher input, or tasks which pupils will pursue individually whilst seated together. If, however, part of the aim of the task is to ensure some degree of group collaboration, then six is too great a number as lines of communication will be too complex and the group is likely to split into two or threes.

Bennett and Dunne's research suggests that groups of four seem to be the most effective as a strategy for encouraging cooperation. For younger children of course, working in pairs may be the most appropriate form of organisation for many activities. Our own observations would suggest that children need a great deal of experience in paired situations before they can work successfully together in larger numbers. There are many instances where working as a pair can be actively encouraged by a teacher, encouraging the development of a range of skills essential for successful cooperative working.

Again there is a distinction to be drawn between a cooperative group activity and grouping for the purposes of classroom management. Attempting to group pupils in fours for the majority of the time would lead to very complex organisation in the classroom. There is no possibility of a teacher successfully sustaining a wide range of activities for a large number of smallish groups. Alexander (1992), in his Leeds study, highlighted very clearly the difficulties of maintaining an over-complex class organisation. This work and the Ofsted follow-up report *Curriculum Organisation and Classroom Practice in Primary Schools* (1993) points very clearly to the conclusion that there should be a limited number of teaching groups to maintain at any one time if the classroom is to be managed effectively.

There is a clear distinction between the situation which involves pupils working simultaneously in a number of curriculum areas, and one in which there is a particular subject focus with a variety of activities being undertaken. In the former – often associated with teaching an integrated day – the demands on a class teacher are considerable. Merely setting up the activities initially can necessitate lengthy explanations, demonstrations and interactions, and can take consider-

(iv) Giving teachers a sense of direction

Teachers need a clear sense of purpose to enable them to make best use of their skills. In some senses the direction is set through a school's curriculum policies or guidelines and there is likely to be clear guidance on, for example, approaches to teaching a particular subject or on a whole school issue such as assessment and record keeping.

All teachers therefore, will be supported by policies developed at whole school level. Equally if not more supportive, will be sharing the task of planning with colleagues. At this stage, a written policy starts to be translated into a means of achieving the required outcomes through planning a range of experiences appropriate to the age and needs of a particular group of pupils. Collaborative planning enables teachers to share skills, experience and expertise and may, in some instances, lead also to a sharing of the task of preparation for, or the teaching of, particular aspects of the planned curriculum.

The main responsibility for effective learning at classroom level lies with an individual teacher. Detailed planning in the short term, as well as having an overall view of the curriculum to be covered in the long term, is critical if a teacher is to be confident about exercising his or her professional responsibility and meeting the needs of pupils.

Planning at any level and at any stage should offer support and guidance to a teacher. It should not be merely a paper exercise to meet the needs outlined above, however necessary or desirable they may be. The key test of any policy or strategy for planning is whether it does offer a sense of direction to a school as a whole and to individual teachers in particular.

Before moving on to the various stages and levels of planning it is important to stress how good planning can help teachers in another way. If planning is reasonably thorough, not only does it provide a view of what will be done, it can also supply a retrospective view of the curriculum and make a significant impact upon record keeping. Planning is not simply a record of what will be covered, it also becomes a record of what has been covered and is therefore useful information for the pupils' next teacher or school. If teachers have a record of work covered then it may go some way to relieving the pressure to record each individual child's curriculum coverage on a series of tick sheets.

The stages and levels of planning

If curriculum planning is to be effective it must operate at different levels. At one level there needs to be agreement across the whole school about certain aspects of the curriculum. This is whole school planning. At another level some decisions can be made by year teams, or Key Stage teams working together on planning work which will occur during a particular academic year. At the final level, there is a teacher's own curriculum planning which may cover anything from one term to one day. This section will provide a planning model which explores the various levels and stages of planning and illustrates a logical step by step process which will go some way to ensuring curriculum planning is effective, manageable and, above all, useful. Figure 3.1 provides an overview of the model and highlights some of the key elements to be considered at each stage of the process.

Whole School Planning

There are particular aspects of curriculum planning and organisation which can only be addressed at school level if a school is to develop a curriculum which is coherent and consistent. The responsibilities for deciding overall policy, strategies and approaches to teaching and learning belong to a school rather than to individual classroom teachers. However, the function of planning at school level must be to support and inform the planning that individual teachers will undertake.

As National Curriculum and assessment arrangements have gradually been implemented, curriculum planning has emerged as a significant and time consuming concern. Few schools will have all the levels and type of planning completely in place, but most will be conscious of the need and be in an almost constant process of curriculum planning and development. The planning of the primary curriculum is becoming increasingly like painting the Forth Bridge: as soon as you have finished it is time to start again. This is not a message of despair, rather it indicates the healthy debate in which most schools are engaged about the quality of their curriculum.

Most schools will be working on developing a variety of curriculum documentation which represents their views about aspects of their work. At the whole school level this documentation is likely to focus upon two distinct areas. The first area which will require decisions being taken at whole school level is concerned with those curriculum issues which have an impact across all subjects and provide the whole curriculum with a sense of purpose and coherence. This area includes particularly the school's approach to assessment procedures, provision for special educational needs, approaches to

STAGES AND LEVELS OF PLANNING

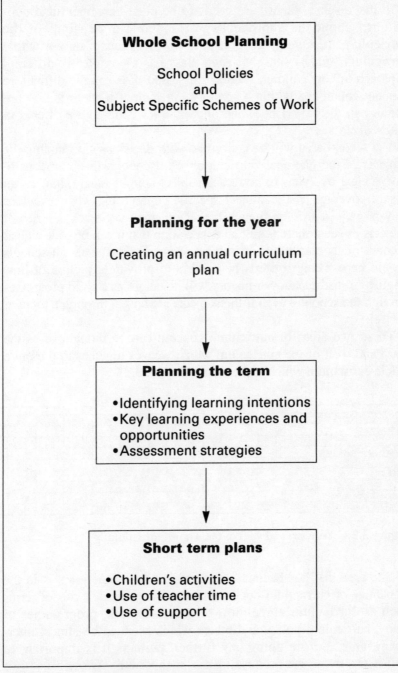

Figure 3.1 – Stages and levels of planning

teaching and learning and equal opportunities. If the whole curriculum, by which we mean everything that the school plans to do, is to make sense, then there needs to be clear agreement and consistency about the approaches to the above dimensions of the curriculum. It is very difficult to see, for instance, how a whole curriculum 'makes sense' if each class has a completely different approach to how children's work is assessed. It is equally difficult to see any coherence within a school's curriculum if there is no consistency in the experiences and opportunities children are offered in different classes.

The second area will be concerned with decisions surrounding the subjects of the National Curriculum. The school will be anxious to have a clear overview of how each subject is to be taught, how it can ensure coverage of the subject specific content and what resources may be required. Even though the school may not teach a series of subjects as such, there is still an expectation that it can provide a clear account of its curriculum in subject terms. For instance, all schools should be working towards being able to provide a picture of how English or mathematics or history will be taught as a child progresses through the school – even if the subjects are taught through a topic or project.

These two areas of curriculum concern can be thought of as the warp and weft of the curriculum which weaves together to present a whole curriculum which makes sense (Figure 3.2).

		En	Ma	Sc	Hist	Geog	Tech	Mu	Art	PE	RE
Assessment											
Teaching and learning											
SEN											
Equal Opportunities											

Figure 3.2 – The warp and weft of the whole curriculum

One area that has become problematical in recent years is in the semantics of curriculum documentation. There are a series of terms such as curriculum guidelines, schemes of work, programmes of study, curriculum policy and others which seem to be almost interchangeable. Before going any further, perhaps it is important to define the terms we propose to use in this book. We will use two terms which we regard as distinct but complementary to each other.

Curriculum policies refer to those elements of the curriculum which have impact across the subjects (the weft of our curriculum). Curriculum policies will provide an overview of the schools approach to particular dimensions of the curriculum (the warp of our curriculum). There is an expectation that schools will have (or be developing) whole school policies covering their approach to areas such as assessment or special educational needs. A SEN policy, for example, may represent the collective decisions of the staff about matters such as:

- How do we define special educational needs?
- What strategies are in place to identify the needs?
- What do teachers do if they identify a pupil with special needs?
- What support/advice mechanisms are available in the school?
- What is the role of parents?
- What involvement will there be from outside agencies? When would they get involved?
- What resources are available?
- Are there any specific requirements concerning record keeping and reviewing progress?

In this way policy promotes consistency across the curriculum. Policy should contain useful information, be helpful to teachers and support them in their own individual planning.

The term we will use to describe the other elements of our curriculum – the warp, is scheme of work. Most schools will be working towards developing schemes of work which cover each subject area. A scheme of work will represent a broad overview of subject entitlement for each pupil in each year group. It will indicate, again in broad terms, what the pupils' experiences in different subjects will be as they progress through the school. A subject scheme of work will provide progression and continuity within each curriculum area so that knowledge and skills within each subject will be developed within a framework for the whole school. How schemes of work are put together will vary between schools but most whole school schemes of work will include the following:

- an overview of the kinds of approaches and broad teaching strategies which have been agreed within each subject;
- outline of content to be covered in each year group and links with National Curriculum;
- subject skills which will be referred to or introduced within each

Data Handling – AT5
Reception

At this stage, the emphasis of data handling experiences should be on:

- sorting according to a wide range of criteria
- encouraging children to describe the criteria used
- discussion of various ways of sorting
- whole class experience of various ways of representing information, including the same information shown in different forms
- discussion of the possible outcomes of a variety of situations.

Experiences Needed	Possible Activities	Resources
Sorting according to various criteria	Sorting into sets according to criteria set by teacher (eg colour, shape)	Transport/animal shapes, house-sorts
	Sorting deciding on own criteria Explaining/labelling sets	Variety of natural objects
	Identifying objects which should not be included and explaining reasons	
Recording with objects/representing information in various ways	Class activity – block graph to show various objects collected on local walk	
	Individual – representing children's favourite foods with blocks	Multilink/unifix cubes
	Discussing information shown on drawings/graphs/in practical form	
Recognising possible outcomes of various events	Class discussions – possible sex of expected baby – possible weather on forthcoming trip – possible end to story	Appropriate opportunities!

Data Handling – AT5 continued

Creating mapping diagrams/discussing then interpreting information	Class activity eg – favourite foods – shoe sizes – holiday destinations	Could be linked with current topic

Year 1

Above experiences should continue, but with development of individual or small group work where class activities have previously been the norm.

There will be increased emphasis on pupils:
– deciding on the criteria to use for various ways of sorting
– devising ways of representing information
– formulating their own questions to gather particular information.

Some activities will be combined, or extended. Particular examples are:

Experiences Needed	**Possible Activities**	**Resources**
Sorting objects and representing results in different ways	Use of Venn diagram/tree diagram	
Organising the collection of data, recording findings	Use of tally charts, transferral of information to create block graph or tree diagram for eg pupils eye colour, number of siblings, favourite stories	
Recognising that some outcomes are uncertain, others certain or impossible	Group activity sorting range of statements into various categories – very likely/unlikely/uncertain	Adult helper

Figure 3.3 – Extract from scheme of work for mathematics

year group;
- suggestions for particular teaching strategies and key experiences to be offered;
- resources available.

Schemes of work will also vary in length and detail. A whole school scheme of work for English, for instance, will be significantly different from that for a foundation subject, as the various strands of English will need to be developed individually as well as in relation to each other. In other words a school may want to document its approach to reading, writing and speaking and listening in some detail, whereas an approach to a foundation subject, whilst being no less rigorous, will be briefer. Figures 3.3 and 3.4 provide examples of parts of two schemes of work.

Scheme of work for history (extract)

YEAR TWO

There are no prescribed History Study Units (HSU) in Year 2. However, all children should continue to develop aspects of historical understanding, although history may not appear as a specific subject on the timetable.

In Year 2 children will explore the following ideas:
- Historical understanding – AT1.
- How the past can be represented in different ways – AT2.
- How they can begin to find out about the past – AT3.

Key experiences/opportunities
- Using artefacts – displaying items which show how things change and develop over time. The school has a store of source items:
  – range of light sources candles —> bedside light
  – small selection of old newspapers and magazines
  – photographs of the local environment.

When artefacts are used children should be encouraged to discuss and identify differences and similarities, sequence objects and/or photos.

Scheme of work for history (extract) continued

- Visits — at least one visit/trip should have an historical element. It can be local – extending the use of the school photograph collection, or further afield. Activities should focus upon the AT1-3.

- Use of stories/ accounts — these are an important resource. Through stories and discussions children should be able to think about real and unreal events, people and their predicaments and motives.

- Use of language — wherever possible maintain the development of historical language.

- Oral history — provide opportunities for pupils to listen to other people telling them about the past.

- Use of time lines — these can be built up – particularly focusing on their own lives, and events over a short period.

- Use current events, special days and festivals.

Available Resources – are held centrally or are available in the library. All the following will be helpful in Year 2.

- Small selection of artefacts.
- Good range of postcards/photographs especially of the locality.
- Teachers support material – available in staff library.
- Reference books – a wide range, but there are some 'boxed' sets which focus upon
  - Toys
  - Children's games
  - Family life.
- Sets of books are also available from the LEA loan services, but these must be ordered at least one term in advance (for advice see co-ordinator).

YEAR THREE

Children will do two HSUs during Year 3

1. Tudors and Stuarts

The following are a range of opportunities and experiences which should be included in planning this history study unit.

- Knowledge of key figures and events during the period. Time line.
- Children should have a chance to focus upon a particular aspect or event of the period. We are quite well resourced in the following areas:
  - Civil War
  - Everyday life (Tudors)
  - Ships and Seafaring (Elizabethan)
  - Art and Entertainment.
- Where appropriate some children should be given a chance to research into particular biographies.
- Stories – historical fiction, a good selection in library.
- Visits – there are several good examples of Tudor buildings in this locality (see the co-ordinator).
- Drama – an effective means of exploring some ideas and events (N.B. AT2).

2. Ships and Seafarers

This unit should develop some of the work in Tudors and Stuarts. All children should have opportunities to:
- Use various pictures, photographs and reproductions to sequence how ships have changed and developed.
- Visits – the Maritime Museum is within striking distance. The museum provides a very good educational service, but it requires careful planning (for details see co-ordinator).
- Time line to show key people and development of ships.
- Groups of pupils can research into different aspects of seafaring. We are well resourced for the following:
  - pirates
  - voyages of discovery
  - slave triangle.

Scheme of work for history (extract) continued

- There are good information books on several key figures.
- Extended Writing – ship's log gives a good opportunity.
- 'Life on board' has some good potential for drama/simulations exploring different perspectives.

Figure 3.4 – Extract from scheme of work for history

The actual time devoted to teaching the various aspects of the curriculum is becoming an increasingly important aspect of curriculum planning. What has been established is that in schools all over the country there is a significant difference in the amount of time spent on actual teaching. This disparity in teaching time in primary schools led to the Department for Education issuing guidelines about how much time should be spent in teaching. The guidelines published in 1990 suggest that at KS1 pupils should have 21 hours teaching, and at KS2 23.5 hours (DFE Circular No. 7/90).

Curriculum time is another way of viewing the whole curriculum and there is a growing expectation that schools will be able to account for their curriculum in amounts of time. There is understandable concern in primary schools that auditing the curriculum in terms of time spent on each subject is very difficult given the cross-subject nature of their curriculum – especially in English. Nevertheless, the expectation is there, and once schools become familiar with this way of looking at the curriculum they may find it useful in their planning. In some respects organising curriculum time is a similar task to organising the 1,265 hours of teacher time. Once the total number of hours is decided, it is a case of allocating time to the various activities.

At whole school level decisions need to be taken about the following:

- What is the total amount of annual teaching time?
- What is the total amount for each term?
- What percentage of time will be allocated to each subject?
- How many actual hours are represented by the percentages?

Once this information is established then teachers doing the next stage of planning can begin to consider their use of curriculum time. In Figure 3.5 we can see some broad allocation of time. Using this information, teachers can begin to think how they use their curriculum time, perhaps keeping in mind that some school terms are longer than others and so the amount of work covered will be different. It also provides all teachers with some guidelines which ensure a significant degree of consistency. For instance, in a school with two or three parallel classes in each year group, it is important that not only do children follow the same schemes of work, but that a similar amount of time is devoted to it over a period of one year. Having a notion of the time available should also help planning to be realistic, particularly as in our experience many teachers plan too much rather than too little. As we move on to the next stage of planning we will be able to see how a school which has developed agreed policies, schemes of work and some idea of how time is allocated can support the work of all teachers.

Planning for the year

If possible, this level of planning should be done with colleagues. At this stage teachers will be looking at all areas of the curriculum, planning and organising the various elements into a coherent annual curriculum plan. A particular task at this stage is to organise the work into various subjects or topics, and look at the timescale for various parts of the curriculum.

In general terms, the curriculum can be divided into three main parts. The first are those areas of the curriculum which should be the subject of constant attention, which would include the core subjects, particularly English and mathematics. There will be very few days when a primary school teacher does not teach some elements of maths or English. The second part of the curriculum are those areas which will form the basis of study for a particular period, perhaps a term or even half of a term. Subjects such as technology, history, geography and art may be the topic focus for a distinct period of time. If we take our nominal time allocations from Figure 3.5, then the 5% history or 5% geography does not necessarily mean that it is 5% of each week. The 5% may be condensed into one or two terms, and thereby be a larger percentage of time within those terms, remembering that balance in subjects should be sought over the academic year, rather than within a term. The third piece of the curriculum jigsaw is those 'fixed' points within the timetable which all teachers must build around. These 'fixtures' would include PE times, games time and possibly things such as radio or TV times. In most schools these 'fixtures' are timetabled centrally and teachers have to plan around them. Working in this way, teachers will be able to organise and map out their annual curriculum plan (Figures 3.6 and 3.7).

The following provides a possible model of whole school curriculum time. It is based upon a school achieving the amount of teaching time per week, recommended in DfE Circular 7/90.

Teaching time for week KS2	23.5 hours
No. of weeks per year	39
No. of weeks per year devoted to special events or occasions	3
Annual total teaching weeks	36
Annual total teaching hours	846
Term One (*13 weeks*)	306
Term Two (*11 weeks*)	259
Term Three (*12 weeks*)	282

Possible subject allocation (to the nearest hour)

		No. of hours per term		
	Annual % time	One	Two	Three
English	25	77	65	71
Mathematics	25	77	65	71
Science	15	46	39	42
Technology	5	15	13	14
History	5	15	13	14
Geography	5	15	13	14
Physical Education	5	15	13	14
Art	5	15	13	14
Music	5	15	13	14
Religious Education	5	15	13	14
		305	260	282

Figure 3.5 – Whole school curriculum time

KS1 Year 1

	Autumn Term (14 weeks)	Spring Term (14 weeks)	Summer Term (11 weeks)
WORK ACROSS THE CURRICULUM Numeracy/Literacy/Reading Speaking and Listening/Handwriting/Spelling/IT			
Timetabled:	PE/Games (1½ hours) Drama (30 mins)	Music (30 mins) PE/Dance (1½ hours)	Timetabled: PE/Swimming (1½ hours)

THEME: Change

Science AT2
Art
English AT3/AT5

History
Technology
Maths AT5

THEME: Myths and Legends

Maths AT4 Shape and Space

Science AT3 – Materials and their properties
Geography AT3 Physical Geography

English AT1/AT2
Art

History
Music

THEME: Places

Geography AT2/AT 4
Science AT4
English AT3

THEME: to be decided after review in Spring Term

Figure 3.6 – Annual curriculum plan

81

KS2 Years 5/6

ON-GOING WORK	
Basic Numeracy / Literacy / Maths (particularly AT1) / Writing Skills / IT	

FIXED LESSONS WEEKLY: 2 x PE sessions + Games   1 x 45 mins Music   1 x 45 mins RE

AUTUMN TERM (14 weeks)		SPRING TERM (11 weeks)		SUMMER TERM (14 weeks)	
1st half	2nd half	1st half	2nd half	1st half	2nd half

PROJECT: Local Study

History
Geography AT2

Art

Technology –
generate
challenge from
local study

PROJECT: Movement

Science

English
AT3/4/5

PROJECT: RE Study

Music

Drama

PROJECT: Developing Country

Geography AT2/Science AT2

Technology   Art

Science AT3
Materials and
their properties

Maths AT4
Shape and
Space

History CSU4

English AT2
 – research skills
 – discussion of a
   variety of texts

Figure 3.7 – Annual curriculum plan

82

As can be seen from the figures, this is a broad picture which will begin to address aspects of subject breadth and balance, as well as the allocation of time. This kind of plan is also helpful since it allows teachers to begin to plan ahead for any specific resources that need to be ordered, or visits to be arranged. Using a plan such as this would also create a sense of confidence through the knowledge of knowing where you are going. Such a plan could be shared with other teachers and possibly parents.

The annual curriculum plan contains various combinations of ongoing subject-specific work, short periods of sharply focused work, and term long topics involving a variety of subject combinations. The plans in figures 3.6 and 3.7 have only indicated the main focus of the project, they do not exclude other areas of work being utilised or introduced. It is inevitable that all projects will have a strong element of English as reading, researching and writing will form a significant part of any project.

For many teachers in primary schools, the most popular form of curriculum organisation has been the topic or project, and there has been a considerable resistance by teachers to adopting a curriculum which is organised and taught along clearly defined subject lines. In reality, most teachers will use a combination of subject teaching and topic work. Topic or project work has some advantages, such as providing a degree of relevance to different subjects. For instance, the study of history and geography can be brought together within the scope of a local study. Topics can also provide a focus for the development of skills particularly in terms of English, art and information technology. Topics are less successful when they do not have a clear focus, and try to make rather tenuous links across different subjects. Trying to get too many different subjects into one topic sometimes leads to learning which is superficial and lacking in quality and depth.

It may be useful at this point to summarise how far we have gone in our planning levels. The school is developing schemes of work which indicate what each year group should be broadly covering, and annual curriculum plans have organised the learning into a series of 'blocks'. The task now is to translate these 'blocks' into manageable units planned in more detail and on a shorter timescale.

Planning the Term

It is at this stage that teachers need to look in some detail at the work they will be doing over the next few weeks. The timescale is flexible, a term may seem too long for detailed planning and some teachers may prefer to work in half terms. It is also useful to bear in mind the difference in the length of terms. In some instances it may be appropriate to plan for a term, in others for half a term. Many schools have common planning formats which are useful in developing a consistent approach to the planning process. If there is no format, then the rest of this section may provide some ideas about what kind of format would be the most suitable.

This medium term planning is concerned to put detail into the curriculum blocks you have identified within the annual curriculum plans. At this point it is important to consider exactly what kind of detail it would be useful to identify. Once again, if there is the possibility of doing this with colleagues this would be advantageous.

In Figure 3.8 we can see a familiar example of teacher planning. It places the topic or project title in the middle of the page and plots the different subject areas around the topic to create the familiar topic web. In this particular example there are some specific curriculum focuses, English, science, history, maths and art. What is also noticeable about this web is the emphasis within each curriculum area on children's activity. What is being planned here, however, is what children will do; there is no direct reference to what children will learn. This distinction is an important one, thrown into sharp focus by the growing importance of assessment. It is becoming more important for teachers to identify learning intentions rather than activities, since this will give them a clearer idea of what should be the focus of their assessments. Put simply, if we are unclear about what the children should be learning, how can we begin to assess whether they have learned it? A planning model which identifies only pupil activity as in Figure 3.8, is no longer sufficient, as it fails to recognise the crucial distinction between doing and learning. There is a second practical reason why teachers at this stage in their planning may find it easier to think about learning intentions rather than activities. It is that to try and plan activities for a term or even half a term would be very time consuming. Learning intentions will not change radically over the medium term as they will be concerned with the development of understanding, knowledge and skills over time. Activities, on the other hand, will change frequently since different activities will focus upon the same learning intentions, and all children need a variety of experience. We therefore need a planning format which extends and develops the 'web', and it is to this that we now turn.

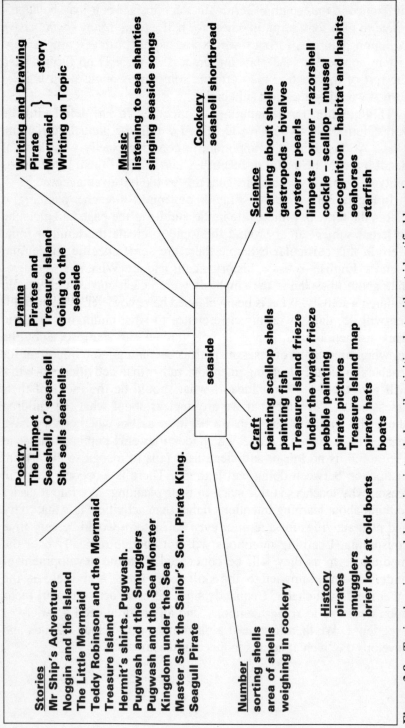

Stories
Mr Ship's Adventure
Noggin and the Island
The Little Mermaid
Teddy Robinson and the Mermaid
Treasure Island
Hermit's shirts. Pugwash.
Pugwash and the Smugglers
Pugwash and the Sea Monster
Kingdom under the Sea
Master Salt the Sailor's Son. Pirate King.
Seagull Pirate

Number
sorting shells
area of shells
weighing in cookery

History
pirates
smugglers
brief look at old boats

Poetry
The Limpet
Seashell, O' seashell
She sells seashells

Craft
painting scallop shells
painting fish
Treasure Island frieze
Under the water frieze
pebble painting
pirate pictures
Treasure Island map
pirate hats
boats

seaside

Drama
Pirates and
Treasure Island
Going to the
seaside

Writing and Drawing
Pirate ⎱ story
Mermaid ⎰
Writing on Topic

Music
listening to sea shanties
singing seaside songs

Science
learning about shells
gastropods – bivalves
oysters – pearls
limpets – ormer – razorshell
cockle – scallop – mussel
recognition – habitat and habits
seahorses
starfish

Cookery
seashell shortbread

Figure 3.8 – Topic planning model showing intended pupil activities, but without identified learning purposes

If we return to the consideration of what kind of detail we want to know, the first and at this stage most important task is to identify the learning intentions. Any discussion of learning intentions will inevitably involve some consideration of how teachers begin to cope with the range of abilities in their classroom. In all classes there may well be a range of learning intentions which will vary according to pupils' abilities. However, a word of caution: any attempt to identify learning intentions for individual pupils is not a practicable proposition (unless a child has very specific needs). On the other hand, it may be appropriate however to identify different learning intentions for different groups of pupils. Having identified learning intentions, it would be useful to make reference to National Curriculum programmes of study and levels of attainment where appropriate, as this will also then serve as a rudimentary record of work covered. It would also be useful to indicate on your planning any specific resource requirements.

How much you plan at this stage in terms of activities is flexible. It would be useful to plan any major or key experiences which you want to offer pupils. This may be expressed as an outcome, for instance the production of a book, a drama, or a display. These learning intentions may be subject specific, such as the introduction of a new mathematical concept, or an understanding about a scientific process. As well as learning intentions related to a specific subject, there are also some experiences or opportunities that it is important for children to have which are not confined to a single subject area. In fact, there are many learning experiences which appear to be common to several of the subject specific National Curriculum orders. Often these intentions are concerned with how children learn, or how they develop a range of learning skills.

Figure 3.9 indicates some of the experiences and opportunities that should be available, but they are not confined to a single subject. For example, if we refer to the section on 'opportunities for talk' we can soon see there a range of particular experiences concerning talk which could be provided through several areas of the curriculum. 'To question and predict' for instance could occur in almost any curriculum area, but nevertheless is a necessary and important skill to develop. It is perhaps worth considering whether the 'planned' curriculum at this stage is one that is balanced in terms of experiences and opportunities as well as subjects.

Before moving on to the next stage it is important at this point to return to the issue of assessment. Assessment is explored in detail in the next chapter, but it is crucial that planning and assessment are

A. LEARNING EXPERIENCES

1.	Opportunities for Talk
a)	To contribute and explain
b)	To question and predict
c)	To discuss
d)	Developing technical accuracy
2.	Opportunities for Recording
a)	In a variety of forms
b)	To organise ideas and information
c)	As part of the learning process
d)	For the purposes of presentation

B. LEARNING OPPORTUNITIES

1	To plan
2	To present
3	Pupil groupings
4	For role play
5	To research

Figure 3.9 – Key Learning Experiences and Opportunities

seen as part of the same process. In the medium term, it is advisable to identify the assessment strategies to be employed to make some judgements about pupils' progress. This, of course, will be made much more manageable as a result of identifying learning intentions.

Having identified the key medium term planning issues it is possible to devise a planning format to include those headings. Figures 3.10 and 3.11 provide examples of a possible format, expanding some subject elements of the theme or project planned for the autumn term in the annual curriculum plan (Figures 3.6 and 3.7). As can be seen, key activities, resources and assessment procedures are listed alongside a series of learning intentions and National Curriculum references.

It may be helpful to again summarise the model so far. We have looked at planning whole school policies, and subject schemes of work. These provide all teachers with an indication of what the curriculum requirements are within each year group. The second level of planning is the medium term in which an outline of the year is put together showing how the curriculum is to be organised, which subjects will be taught discretely, and which will be part of a theme or topic. The annual curriculum plan can also be used to monitor the subject balance. This is followed by a breakdown of the current term where it is vital that teachers identify the main learning intentions. The next step is to look at the short term planning which will support the daily business of teaching and learning.

Short term plans

What teachers understand as short term planning will vary, but for the purposes of this book we are referring to planning on a weekly or two-weekly basis. This level of planning is about having some clear ideas about how children and the teacher are going to be spending each day. For that reason we propose a format which provides for daily planning and gives a weekly overview (Figure 3.12). Figure 3.13 provides an example of what might appear on this type of daily plan.

Essentially this short term planning is a teaching diary, intended to translate the medium term plans into practical activity. The concerns of short term planning are different to those of the previous stages. These are no longer broad overviews, but the nitty-gritty of what needs to be thought about to ensure that teaching and learning are effective. The learning intentions will not alter radically from week to week, so they will not be a major concern here. However, unlike the medium term planning, in the short term what the children will do is

KS1 Autumn Term Theme – 'Change' Focus – Science/Art (first half-term)

Learning intentions	National Curriculum Reference	Key Activities/Experiences	Resources	Assessment Strategies
Observe and discuss changes in the environment.	Sc AT1 A AT2	Visits to local woods to look at autumnal changes (early Sept-late Oct). Discussion of representation of seasons in various artists' work	Project books collection 'Autumn'. Take photographs in woods. Postcards, books, prints for display.	Ability to observe accurately, ask questions, predict change (individual).
Understand that change can be effected in various ways.	Sc AT3	Cooking. Study of water cycle. Discussion of the effects of weathering.	Parent helpers. Water cycle chart. Collection of rocks/stones, etc.	Pupils' representation and explanation of water cycle (individual).
Investigate ways of changing materials.	Sc AT3 A AT1	Explore the effect of heating on dough and clay – of light on various materials. Papers. Colour mixing – autumnal scenes.	Parent helpers. Powder paints/ various papers.	
Begin to understand the process of natural change.	Sc AT2	Development of ourselves - effects of growth, importance of food and exercise. Study the effects of decay on various materials.	Growth charts, photographs, healthy eating charts. Collection of cans, vegetable waste.	'Growth books' (individual).
Review, discuss and modify work.	A AT1	Class discussion on our representations of autumn – focus on ways of improving scenes and try them out.	Children's pictures.	Observation and notes of discussion (class). Individual pieces of work before/after.

Figure 3.10 – Medium Term Planning Format

KS2 Autumn Term Local Study Subject Focus – History/Geography (second half-term)

Learning intentions	National Curriculum Reference	Key Activities/Experiences	Resources	Assessment Strategies
Geography Introduce concept of land use and reasons for variety. Develop mapping skills further – directions, variety of scale. Representing information on maps. Awareness of geographical features of their home region. *History* Be aware of how the locality has changed. Develop skills of using evidence. Gain knowledge about local history. Be able to identify and sequence local buildings. Focus particularly on development post 1930.	AT1 L1/2/3 AT2 L1/2/3/4 AT1 L2/3/4 AT2 L2/3 AT3 L2/3/4	Produce local trail using photographs to show sites of historical significances. Plot land use on map. Invite local people to talk about their experiences. Prepare interviews. Use variety of historical sources – photos, newspapers. Use of time lines. Debate a current issue, e.g. planning dispute.	Photos/newspapers. Visitors. Tape recorder. Camera.	Knowledge quiz. Judge outcomes. Discussion in groups. Observation of debate.

Figure 3.11 – Medium Term Planning Format

Monday	Tuesday	Wednesday	Thursday	Friday
Activities	*Activities*	*Activities*	*Activities*	*Activities*
Use of Adults	*Use of Adults*	*Use of Adults*	*Use of Adults*	*Use of Adults*
Teacher focus	*Teacher focus*	*Teacher focus*	*Teacher focus*	*Teacher focus*
Resources	*Resources*	*Resources*	*Resources*	*Resources*

Figure 3.12 – Short term planning – Daily planning sheet (*This represents an A3 sized sheet*)

Monday	Tuesday
Activities	
Session 1 – **Maths**	
Whole Class – differentiated speed tests (10-15 mins)	
Group A - Consolidate work on fractions/maths scheme (p.62-65)	
Group B - Consolidate work as place value (p.37-41) HTU	
Group C - Maths investigation (group task), place value	
Group D - Practise bonds up to 20, then: introduce ½ ¼ + work (p.15)	
Session 2 – **Paired Reading: PE** (Whole Class)	
5 mixed groups – Developing and refining sequences – get some discussions going	
Session 3 – **Project – Local Study**	
Whole Class – review work so far –	
'3' mixed groups/3 tasks and rotate	
a. Write up visit	
b. Photo sequencing (in 2s)	
c. Plot land use on street map (in 3s)	
Use of adults	
Assistance – 20 min periods	
Mr Jones – Session 3: Working with task b.	
Teaching Focus	
Session 1 Group B (15 mins), Group D (15 mins)	
Session 2 Listen to Sophie/Dan/Tariq	
Session 3 Task c. Classifications/Why and how?	
Resources	
Photographs	
Maths – fraction material	

Figure 3.13 – Example of daily plan

important so some thought should be given to the range of activities which will be offered each day. It is inevitable that when considering the nature and range of activities other aspects of classroom organisation and management will have to be taken into account. Decisions will have to be taken at this stage about the following:

Differentiation:
- Which activities will be appropriate for everyone?
- Will some activities be designed for specific groups?

Pupil Organisation
- What is the most appropriate form of organisation for the activity?

Extra support
- How will the classroom assistant be used?
- What is the role of any parent helpers?

Decisions about the above will have to be made on a short term, sometimes daily basis.

Perhaps, however, the most important element of the short term planning is the use of teacher time. Teacher time is the most important resource in every classroom and therefore its use must be carefully planned. There should be time specifically allocated for teaching, assessing and monitoring, otherwise time will disappear, and the role of the teacher may become that of someone being reactive rather than proactive.

The introduction of the National Curriculum has lead to an improvement in teachers' planning. The key concern we have tried to address is how can planning be manageable, useful and effective? As we said earlier, good planning will not guarantee good teaching, but most good teaching is well-planned. A well-planned curriculum will serve many purposes: it will ensure that all children receive their entitlement; it will provide for breadth and balance, and continuity and progression; but perhaps most importantly it will help teachers to keep control of their teaching, and it may actually result in time being available for some of those spontaneous moments that cannot be planned for, but often lead to the most exciting and productive learning.

The Ofsted report on *Curriculum Organisation and Classroom Practice* (1993) identified the following factors as being associated with successful topic work in classrooms:

- an agreed, consistent system of planning;
- whole school agreement about subject coverage and the balance between subjects and topics;
- a degree of cooperation in planning;
- account taken of National Curriculum requirements;
- planning focused on learning outcomes, activities and assessment.

In this chapter we have endeavoured to highlight some of the main principles which underlie successful approaches to curriculum planning. Schools which have an agreed, common structure to their planning will provide a clear frame of reference for class teachers, and teachers planning together within year groups or key stages will ensure a consistent and coherent approach to the curriculum. Planning based on clear purposes, identifying learning intentions, will help to ensure appropriate provision of activities and will form the basis of assessment of pupils' progress and achievements.

Effective planning should be clearly staged, and follow a logical route with one stage building on another. Again, we have tried to demonstrate some routes through these various stages in order to ensure that planning is manageable and effective in supporting the work of the class teacher.

Starting Points

The Need for Planning
- Does your planning reflect your long term aims?
- Who do you share your planning with?

The Stages and Levels of Planning
- What would you consider are the key features of good planning?
- In what ways could children be involved in curriculum planning?

CHAPTER 4
Assessment, Recording and Reporting

Assessment, recording and reporting are usually linked together because unless an assessment has been made, it is difficult to imagine what can be recorded or reported. However, there is a very significant distinction between assessment on the one hand and recording and reporting on the other. Assessment is an integral part of the practice of teaching and learning whilst recording and reporting are systems by which information is stored or transferred. In other words, assessment will have an impact upon children's learning and teachers' teaching in a much more fundamental way than recording and reporting. Because of this significant distinction, the chapter will focus initially upon assessment followed by recording and reporting.

Assessment

In recent years, the assessment of children's learning has assumed a high profile, due to the controversial nature of government proposals. There is general agreement amongst teachers, parents and politicians that it is important to assess children's learning. What there is less agreement about, and what has been the focus of the controversy, is the precise nature of the assessment process.

Essentially, there are two forms of assessment. The first type is concerned with finding out at some given point what children do or do not know, and what they can or cannot do. Because this form of assessment occurs at the end of a particular period and is usually designed to assess the learning within that period, it is referred to as summative assessment. In short, it is an attempt to summarise learning and achievement at a particular point.

The second type of assessment is concerned with making more frequent assessments about learning and subsequently making adjustments to the curriculum, based upon those judgements. This type of assessment is formative in that it has an impact upon the nature and range of the curriculum children are offered. The problem, as the Government has discovered, is that it is very difficult to design a system of assessment which is both summative and formative. The reason for the high profile of assessment is the debate about which of these elements should be emphasised. If the emphasis lies in summative assessment, then the nature of the assessment is such that it occurs at particular, designated times and it does not necessarily inform what the future pattern of a pupil's learning may be. Statutory assessments at ages 7 and 11 are representative of a summative assessment process. Summative assessment is an important element in any assessment system and provides some valuable information for parents and teachers in the next Key Stage. The problem arises of course, if, for example, a child at the end of Key Stage 2 is assessed by the statutory tests and tasks as being able to do very little, but who may have spent a considerable amount of time on a curriculum which has demonstrably been ineffective. It is for this reason that most teachers see the need for a more formative, continuous mode of assessment which informs children's future learning experience.

This continuous, formative type of assessment is increasingly known as teacher assessment. What is generally recognised is that any efficient assessment system needs to employ strategies which are both summative and formative: there should be some fixed points at which children's learning is assessed, but also in between those fixed points there needs to be an efficient and effective system of teacher assessment which informs the types of opportunities and experiences provided for pupils on a regular basis. It is also important to bear in mind that because there can be as much as four years between the fixed points, it is likely that schools themselves will want to introduce some assessment strategies which share many characteristics of the summative tasks and tests.

There is currently no clearly established picture of the statutory tasks and tests that will occur in the primary years and there may not be for some time. However, those teachers in school directly engaged in administering statutory tasks and texts in Years 2 and 6 will be provided with annual guidance and support from the Schools Curriculum and Assessment Authority (SCAA) to help them to fulfil the requirements at the ends of Key Stages 1 and 2. We intend to focus a little more closely on how all teachers can develop strategies in their classrooms and the development of a consistent approach across a school.

Whole School Approach

Assessment is an area in which consistency across a school is vital. Consistency is important to ensure that teachers make similar judgements when confronted with similar evidence, it is important in reporting judgements to parents to ensure that they do not receive conflicting information, and it is important for pupils that teachers are consistent in their expectations. The only way to achieve such a degree of commonality is to develop and sustain a whole school approach to all aspects of assessment.

There is an expectation that all schools will have, or be developing, a school assessment policy. This policy should address the following issues:

- how is pupil progress and achievement assessed?
- are assessments consistent across the school?
- what impact does assessment have upon learning?
- how does the school record progress and achievement?
- how is achievement reported?

All these issues need careful thought and discussions.

In addressing these issues, there are certain aspects of assessment which, if tackled on a school basis, will help with the development of a consistent approach. The first aspect of assessment is a strategy for marking pupils' work. Marking work is an activity which is engaged in by all teachers, but there is often considerable variation in how it is done. Any school marking policy must recognise that it is unreasonable to expect all the work produced by pupils to be given the same attention. On some occasions work produced will only need a brief look, whilst on others the outcome may be subjected to some scrutiny. In these instances, there needs to be some agreement on how teachers will respond to the work and this should form part of the whole school policy. For example, pieces of work which cover a range of skills and knowledge, such as a project or topic folder, could be marked and annotated in such a way as to recognise specific achievement over several areas, by using National Curriculum attainment targets. Future learning targets would also be indicated. This would mean that marking, in this sense, is a significantly different activity from the cursory tick at the end of a piece of work. On some occasions, the final outcome may not be the focus of the assessment, and so marking a piece of work may not be appropriate. What is important however, is that marking, if done effectively, can serve several purposes. For children, marking could both recognise and acknowledge their achievements and provide them with written targets at which to aim in the future. For teachers, effective marking can provide a good record of pupil progress, and form a continually developing evidence base on which final end-of-year judgements can be made, and if necessary, justified.

The second aspect connected with marking is ensuring a degree of consistency when making judgements. Essentially, the question to ask is: how can a school ensure with some certainty that pupils in different classes are being judged according to the same criteria? Is there uniformity in the judgements being made by different teachers? One way in which a school, or a small group of teachers perhaps in a year group, can develop some consistency is through moderating pieces of work and trying to reach agreement about the judgements they make. This is a very effective way of developing the kind of marking strategy outlined previously.

The moderating procedure would involve a series of quite brief meetings in which teachers discuss specific pieces of work and try to reach some agreement about the judgements they would make, and be prepared to say why they would make those judgements. In the initial stages it may be more appropriate to use pieces of work (representing a range of levels of attainment) which are entirely anonymous, so that teachers do not feel a need to defend the work. At the same time teachers can also discuss how they would annotate or mark the work, thereby developing the marking system. The annotated pieces of work which have been the subject of the discussion can be stored centrally, and be used as a reference point by all teachers to support them in their own judgements. This 'school portfolio' will also serve as evidence that the school has made some determined efforts to develop a consistent approach in making judgements about pupils' work.

Before moving into a more detailed look at managing effective classroom strategies for assessment, it is important that we reinforce the relationship between curriculum planning and assessment. The importance of this relationship should be evident from the previous chapter, but it cannot be overemphasised. Effective assessment is an integral part of teaching and learning and it is vital for effective learning. The issues of matching work to children's abilities can only be tackled through careful assessment. Teachers determined to move a child 'from the known to the unknown' as the saying goes, requires a knowledge of the child's known. Assessment, in some form, is therefore a prerequisite of effective teaching, and relates to curriculum planning in very fundamental ways. Firstly, planning needs to be done on the basis of some assessment by a class teacher, although in the early stages of a school year it may well be based on information from a previous teacher. Secondly, planning in the medium term should have clear learning intentions, as otherwise it will be unclear precisely what is to be assessed. Thirdly, because assessment is so important, time should be planned for it in the short term. Our experience suggests that unless time is allowed for assessment, it is unlikely to occur in the purposeful way in which it should. Following on from this we can now focus upon the nature of assessment, recording and reporting in the classroom.

Teacher Assessment

Just as effective teaching is usually underpinned by good planning, effective planning is based on close assessment of children's learning needs. Whilst assessment has statutory endorsement, and is therefore a formalised process at certain points in a child's education (notably at the end of each Key Stage), teacher assessment is a continual process and a key factor in managing teaching and learning. The fundamental reason for assessment is to enable children to learn effectively, and a major challenge for class teachers is managing this task on a day to day basis. Assessment arising from normal classroom activities will enable a teacher to plan appropriately to meet a range of differing needs. Developing a range of skills and strategies for arrangement in the course of those activities is an important part of the teacher's role.

Many teachers will claim, with justification, that they were assessing children long before the onset of National Curriculum. Whilst this may be the case, assessment in this context tends to imply general observation of the activities of a class or individuals and the gathering of a range of information about pupils' behaviour, attitudes and interactions, sometimes almost by osmosis. Focusing on the actual learning taking place has been less developed, and so there is a sense in which teachers have needed to refine their range of skills to enable them to look closely at this area. There are two essential elements here. First is the need for assessment to be focused, and the second is the need to plan for it to take place. A teacher will need to be very clear about three areas:

* what will be assessed;
* who will be assessed;
* when assessment will take place.

It is important to remember that you cannot assess all of the children all of the time. For this reason, a planned system of assessment will enable the systematic gathering of information about all children as they are engaged in a variety of activities over a period of time.

There are two main aspects to teacher assessment which need to be carefully planned and managed. The first is concerned with collecting information and evidence, and making judgements about children's competences and needs. The second aspect is making decisions about the actual use of the information generated and developing systems for recording and retaining evidence of children's progress.

Collecting information and making judgements
On a day to day basis, teachers will use three main strategies for collecting information on children's learning. These are:

- *observing* children engaged in particular tasks;
- *listening* to their responses to a task and engaging in discussion about them;
- *looking* at what they have produced at the end of an activity.

At times, of course, more than one of these approaches may be used, and in certain instances all three will be combined in coming to an overall judgement on children's achievements. There may be times also when arriving at those judgements will take some time, and it may be critical that with some tasks, or for certain children, sufficient time is allowed for decisions to be reached on children's responses to and engagement with a particular activity. Each of the three approaches to collecting information will now be considered in turn.

Observation. Because the emphasis in most classrooms is on activity, it is difficult for some teachers to be comfortable with the notion of 'observing' rather than 'doing' in the classroom. Developing the skills to focus on what is actually happening with children in the course of a task, rather than monitoring its progress or intervening in it, requires a particular discipline and some planning. The key element in classroom observation is that of *focus*. It is important to be clear about which particular tasks will be observed or which individual or groups of children. It is equally important to be clear about what evidence you will be looking for in the course of the observation which might indicate learning response or achievement.

There are various strategies which teachers are using successfully to plan and record observational assessments. Use of observation schedules which can be pre-prepared and photocopied can be helpful in providing an aide-memoire for such assessments. Figures 4.1 and 4.2 provide examples of possible formats for group and individual

Date:				
Subject/Activity:				
Children observed	Aim of task	Approach to task	Observation	Evaluation/ Implications

Figure 4.1 – Group observation sheet

Name:		Date:	
Activity/Learning Context	Focus of observation	Observational notes	Next step in learning

Figure 4.2 – Individual observation sheet

observation. Planning for classroom observation on a short term basis as part of the weekly planning cycle will enable teachers to manage the use of time for observation. A teacher could decide to focus on a certain area of the classroom or a particular task over a 2 to 3 day period, or may decide to focus on certain children in the course of a range of activities over a day. Whatever the nature of the observations planned, being clear about the information which is being sought is critical in enabling the limited time which will be available for this form of assessment to be used most profitably.

There is no real purpose in collecting information which you already have, so for each aspect of classroom observation it is worth clarifying exactly what you, as a teacher, need to know. You may, for example, wish to gather information on some of the following:

- children's ability to use particular skills;
- children's strategies for acquiring and processing particular information;
- children's knowledge or understanding in particular areas;
- children's abilities to participate in a group task.

Whichever area you choose to observe, there is likely to be some specific information which you will seek, but there may also be some incidental information which you will gather and which would be significant in terms of planning future tasks. Just because the incidental evidence was not part of the initial focus does not mean that it can be ignored! With regard to individual children, observation over a period of time will yield some specific information on progress and development. Again, there is no point in gathering information which you already have, so it is worth considering the information which you think it is important to record over a period of time. The nature of this will vary between individual children.

Listening and discussion. Given that most teachers are almost compulsive talkers in the classroom, the very act of listening rather than leading or participating may involve a particular type of self-discipline! It is one which may well be worth developing however, as listening has tremendous potential for acquiring a range of information on children's responses and approaches to particular tasks. It may take a little while to develop the use of this particular strategy in the classroom, not only for the reason cited above, but also because the very act of a teacher joining a group with the intention of 'listening in' may be a new experience for children. Almost inevitably they will expect some guidance, instruction, comment or questions from the teacher as these are aspects of the role with which they will be familiar. For this reason, a teacher may need to be quite explicit with the children about the intention of acting as a listener and it may be helpful to discuss some of the information gathered in this situation with them at the end of the activity. Through doing this, the teacher can combine the task of assessment with the opportunity to reflect back to the children some observations on their achievements in a particular task.

As with observations, listening will require a particular focus. In order to assess learning outcomes, you, as the teacher, will need to be quite clear about learning intentions. Only if these are defined will it be possible to make some judgements about exactly what is being achieved in the course of the task. Listening, combined with observation, creates excellent opportunities for making notes on individual children or particular tasks. Again, being clear about what you want, or need to know, will help to focus the note making and will avoid the temptation to write for the sake of doing so!

Engaging in discussion with pupils may be a planned activity or may develop from what was initially a period of listening. Making some initial notes about key points which you want to explore with individuals or a group will enable the discussion to have a clear structure, and, again, those points should be related to what you need to explore with the children in order to gain further information. There is no doubt that talking something through with children will enable you to gain a good perspective of their level of understanding and any difficulties which they may be experiencing. It is worth spending some time considering the sorts of questions which you might wish to raise in particular situations, so that discussion does not become merely question and answer (although you may want to use that technique to, for example, test pupils' degree of knowledge in a subject). If you wish to elicit information on the development of certain concepts or understanding of particular processes, then a discussion which combines some open questions with some statements, speculations, hypothesising and suggestions will be more revealing as an assessment strategy.

Looking at outcomes. As with observing and listening, looking at the final products of a task involves more than just monitoring whether children have attained what you, or they, intended. As we discussed in the last chapter, the nature of an activity should be determined by the planned learning intention and the product will therefore represent something of what children have achieved in their learning.

It is important to be clear that this representation of achievement may be quite limited, particularly for younger children, and, for this reason, outcomes may need to be assessed in conjunction with other information. Some earlier observation or discussion, even if very brief, will enhance the judgements that are being made and may even be essential to gain a complete picture of the process which the piece of work represents. Having stated that, reviewing outcomes can give a teacher some useful information in a number of areas. These might include:

- a pupil's depth of knowledge in a particular subject;
- the ability to organise information and present it in a new form;
- strategies for recording particular types of information or data;
- the ability to write in different forms for different purposes;
- the ability to evaluate a particular process or artefact;
- achievements in the form of presentation in areas such as drama;
- oral, pictorial or written forms which represent a pupil's understanding.

Deciding, whether to observe, discuss or look at pieces of work, or whether to combine one or more of these will depend to some extent on a teacher's particular teaching style, preferred method of classroom management and the context within which the teacher is working. Having said that, all of the approaches outlined above should be used on some occasions in every classroom. Each will yield a differing perspective on children's learning, and will demand differing skills on the part of the teacher. There is a sense in which one can only get better at the task of managing focused assessment in the classroom through actually doing it. A planned approach to assessment, which will include all children and a range of subjects and learning experiences over a period of time, will help to ensure that the task is manageable and useful to the child and the teacher.

In addition to planning a variety of approaches to assessment and to planning for appropriate use of teacher time to manage the process, there is a need to consider how the children are to be involved. Being open with them about the need for assessment and the ways in which the teacher will be engaged in this task will help them to help you when you are in the process of assessing. It would also be appropriate to share with them the criteria for what is being assessed and how the teacher is to arrive at certain judgements on children's achievements. The more the children understand what your expectations are, the more they will be able to focus on the important elements in a specific task which are fundamental to achieving a satisfactory learning outcome.

Using information and developing assessment systems
As demonstrated above, teachers will need to collect a wide variety of information about children's achievements and needs in a number of varied situations to assess learning over a period of time. There are various means for noting information initially, and whether you use one particular strategy or a variety will depend on personal preference

and the nature of the classroom in which you are working. Teachers are successfully using a variety of methods for recording information quickly. These include:

- a notebook specifically used for assessment purposes;
- a card index system with a card for each child on which to note significant details;
- a small tape recorder or dictaphone for an oral commentary;
- 'post-its' to make quick notes which can be transferred to an assessment file or record system at a later stage.

As with so many aspects of classroom management, finding some ways of making quick notes on pupils' activities may mean some compromises. It will not be possible to record in detail, and it is totally unnecessary to repeat information which you already have. The key message here is that you need to note only significant information about children's levels of understanding, competences or needs. This will often mean a few words about the approach a child has taken to a particular task, or the words which the child uses which demonstrate an important gain or gap in learning.

Whatever method is used, information initially noted will need to form part of a system for building up a complete picture of a child's learning and development. In addition to observations, some evidence of achievement *over a period of time* will be needed to demonstrate pupil progress. The way in which this is managed will depend to some extent on individual school policy. In a number of schools it will take the form of some kind of individual portfolio containing a range of work, teacher observations and notes collected during the time the child attends the school. If this is to provide a comprehensive picture of a child's progress, each piece of work within the portfolio needs to be annotated so that the context of the task and evidence of learning are clear. This may be done in various ways, one of which is shown in Figure 4.3.

As with pupil observation, the key element in the selection of work for something like a portfolio is deciding what is significant for individual pupils. There is little point in photocopying work which is contained in another system, such as a story in an English book or an account of an experiment in a science notebook. If these are significant, reference could be made to them elsewhere, such as on a pupil's record sheet.

If examples of work within a portfolio are carefully selected, clearly annotated and used to show progress over time, they can

ANNOTATION SHEET

SCHOOL

NAME

DATE OF WORK

LEARNING INTENTION

WHAT WAS THE TASK?

WORK PRODUCED BY	Group ☐ Individual ☐
ADULT HELP	None ☐ Some ☐ Considerable ☐
STAGE OF DRAFTING	
TIME SCALE	
N.C. A.T.s	

WHAT DOES THE WORK DEMONSTRATE?

TEACHER'S/PUPIL'S COMMENTS (optional)

FUTURE TARGET?

Figure 4.3 – Example of annotation sheet

provide a useful component of the assessment process. Pupils can be involved in the selection of work themselves, can be helped to see what they are achieving and can become engaged in reviews of achievements and planning of future targets. All of these will depend on appropriate teacher guidance and discussions to enable pupils to develop some skills in self-evaluation. Whilst the variety of work contained within a portfolio should reflect the range of the curriculum, it is important that it also reflects the balance of the curriculum and that particular regard is paid to maintaining a good selection of work which demonstrates achievement within the basic skills. Portfolios can also provide a useful focus for discussion in the course of parent consultations. A selected range of work over a period of time can be extremely effective in demonstrating pupil progress and achievement.

There are, however, certain difficulties inherent in a portfolio or similar system. Making an appropriate selection of material and trying to ensure that it represents the curriculum for each pupil in a class may prove a time consuming and burdensome task, which can easily become an end in itself rather than a means to an end. It can become a system which is quite divorced from anything else happening in the classroom, so whilst it may be a routine task to add work to a portfolio, it may be quite separate from other tasks and be isolated from the child concerned. The whole business of finding time to manage portfolios and organising a suitable system for storage which is going to make them accessible to pupils can present real difficulties for class teachers.

There are some alternatives to a portfolio system which may serve the same purpose of providing evidence of progress over a period of time. One of the most effective of these is a marking strategy similar to the one referred to earlier in this chapter which would include a commentary on the significant elements within a particular piece of work, in a similar way to the annotation sheet previously shown. This approach ensures that evidence of achievement will remain an integral part of a child's work, tracking progress through a series of observations on pieces of work covering various areas of the curriculum.

Another possibility is to use something like a monthly record of unaided writing. This may be in the form of a book in which a child can write freely on a subject of his or her choice. Once again, over a period of time this can form a significant part of a record of progress and the development of a range of skills in written work.

Work which represents achievements in a range of areas can also provide valuable evidence of pupil learning. This might include book-making or a project folder in which pupils will be using a range of knowledge and skills across various subjects to produce an end product. As with other approaches, it is the commentary or annotation which is important in clarifying the significance of the evidence.

Whatever approach may be used, retaining some evidence of learning over a period of time is one aspect of ongoing teacher assessment. This needs to be combined with other information, such as records of structured classroom observations, informal notes on developing attitudes and skills, and the teacher's own professional judgements on individual pupils. The latter element is particularly important as much evidence of pupil learning, particularly but not exclusively, for younger pupils is of an ephemeral nature and whilst notes can be made on some aspects of this no teacher will be in a position to record everything.

Since information on pupil learning will be generated in a variety of ways, it is important to ensure that time is planned for review and evaluation of the developing picture of each individual child. At regular intervals, and a termly basis would seem to be appropriate, teachers need to sift through the various notes they have on pupils and the samples of work collected, in whatever form. This review should focus on key aspects of pupil learning:

- general level of achievement;
- evidence of developing knowledge and concepts;
- development and application of a range of skills;
- attitudes and approaches to learning;
- particular competences, weaknesses and needs.

A brief summary of development in these areas can be used to further inform teacher planning. There will also be some information on attainment which should serve to inform and assist with the completion of pupil records.

Recording

The next two brief sections are distinct from assessment in that they are concerned essentially with managing the information generated by assessment, and passing it on to whoever may need it.

All schools will have some form of record keeping system and teachers will for the most part be expected to keep records up to date. All schools must keep a record of a child's progress through the National Curriculum, and many schools have interpreted this as having to record progress against every statement of attainment. Whilst some teachers and schools may find this useful (although burdensome), it is not a statutory requirement. Pupils' own work and records related to programmes of study, or even profile components, may suffice to show progress and achievement within National Curriculum subjects. The nature of the pupils' records may vary, but most will have some form of tick sheet, often referring to National Curriculum attainment targets, or perhaps programmes of study. Many schools will also have some regime of testing and pupils' marks will be systematically recorded. It is worth mentioning that the strategies outlined earlier in the chapter about marking and annotating pupils' work will also serve as a record of assessment.

Teachers will need to become familiar with their school's record keeping systems especially with regard to the following:

- what has to be recorded;
- how records have to be completed;
- how much evidence has to be kept;
- how the system is to be managed.

Leaving the job of completing all records until the end of term, or half-term, could present teachers with quite an onerous task. It is perhaps advisable to incorporate record keeping into the assessment system so that again, rather than becoming a task distinct from teaching and learning, it becomes part of the process. This may mean that when looking at particular pieces of work, as well as commenting on the work and perhaps annotating it, a teacher can also tick a record sheet if it is appropriate. Methods of recording will to some extent depend on what is being assessed, so that for instance notes on an observation, or resulting from a discussion, may be entered on to a record card or teacher's record book.

The question of how much evidence to keep can present some difficulties. These are the things to bear in mind. Firstly, teachers need evidence which will indicate children's current achievements over the breadth of the curriculum. Secondly, it is important that evidence is kept which indicates children's progress, and this means keeping some work which is dated and annotated. The period of time which this work needs to cover will depend upon the age and ability of each child. Young children may demonstrate significant progress over a relatively short space of time, perhaps a few weeks. Some children towards the end of Key Stage 2 may only show significant progress over several months. Those teachers who will be making end of Key Stage assessments should be particularly careful to maintain a range of up-to-date evidence which supports and illustrates the levels of attainment attributed to each child.

Recording is an important element in teacher assessment but it has proved problematical as many teachers have felt swamped by the amount of paperwork. It is important to keep a sense of perspective and bear in mind that there is no statutory requirement to record achievement against every statement of attainment, and that teachers are entitled to, indeed expected to, use their own professional judgement. Finally in this brief section, it is right that we should also remind ourselves that one piece of work can provide evidence for more than one subject.

Reporting

This is the third piece of the assessment jigsaw, and is closely allied with recording. It is another aspect of management of information, focusing as it does on how teachers communicate their assessments to the various constituents who require the relevant information.

In the majority of cases there are two distinct audiences. Firstly, the professional audience of colleagues, either within the same school or the next phase, will require information about the pupils they are receiving. Secondly, and this is where the main focus of reporting has been, parents are entitled to regular information about their children's progress.

Most schools will have a system for the transfer of information between year groups and other schools. For the most part this will include information about achievement, but also about subject or curriculum coverage. This also provides some opportunities to ensure continuity and progression within the curriculum. There is, of course, no substitute for a face to face discussion about individual pupils, but for those teachers providing information, discussion is aided considerably if there are notes or records to which they can refer.

An important point to make about the transfer of information between teachers is that if assessment is taken seriously, then the information it generates should also be treated seriously. Those teachers who claim a preference not to look at previous records but to 'get to know the children for myself' are doing the children and their colleagues a considerable disservice.

Legislation makes it quite clear that all schools must provide an annual report to parents which indicates their children's progress in the subjects of the National Curriculum. When children reach the end of each Key Stage, the annual report should also indicate a level of achievement in mathematics, English and science. This level will be the result of statutory assessments which include testing, prescribed tasks and teacher assessment. It is only at the end of Key Stages that teachers need to report levels.

Most schools will have recently reviewed their report formats to ensure that they fulfil the latest statutory requirements. As well as providing a report which comments upon achievements in subjects, the majority of schools will also be anxious to provide an overall picture of a child's capabilities. When writing the annual report, a good record system which has been built up and developed over the previous year will provide a good source of reference. Information about various aspects will be readily to hand so that teachers are able to comment on things such as cross-curricular skills, attitudes to work and others, ability to concentrate and cooperate and other areas which do not fit easily into a subject-based report. A card index system, or a teaching diary in which a teacher has noted observations or discussions should provide most of the information required.

As part of the statutory requirements, schools must also indicate that parents can discuss the annual report if they wish. In fact most schools will provide at least one occasion, usually towards the end of the school year, when parents can come and discuss their child's achievements. It is useful to bear in mind when writing reports that, although they need to be clear and informative, they should also form the basis for a discussion, and there is therefore an assumption that the remarks in the report can be expanded.

The reports must provide an honest account of a child's performance, but at the same time be positive. The tone of the writing can make a significant difference. If a report is simply a catalogue of things a child cannot do or finds difficult, then it could be damaging to a child's self-esteem and may give an impression to parents that the school sees children in a negative way. There is always something positive to write about pupils, even if they find learning difficult and have made little progress. The most helpful types of school report give an indication of what has been achieved both socially and academically and also indicate some targets or areas which should be the focus of some future work. The unwritten rule for reports is that they should be positive, but above all else they should not be surprising! If parents find out for the first time in June or July that their child has been disruptive in class, made very little progress in learning and is rather unpopular, then there is something seriously wrong with the communication system between the school and home.

Perhaps the final thing to say about annual reports is that this is one occasion when presentation is very important. For any remarks about progress, or otherwise, to carry weight they must be well written, spelt correctly and look professional. For some teachers the advent of word processing may be just the thing. There have been embarrassing occasions when parents have struggled gainfully but unsuccessfully to decipher a comment about their child's handwriting!

Of all the recent developments in primary education, the focus on assessment is perhaps the most exciting. Effective assessment of pupils' needs supports and refines teaching and learning, and can promote the provision of a curriculum responsive to those needs in quite specific ways. Assessment is not yet another demand on teachers' time, it is fundamental to all their activities and is the foundation of effective teaching.

Starting Points

Assessment
- What do you think constitutes evidence of children's learning and how can you begin to collect it?
- How can teachers begin to ensure 'consistency of judgements'?

Recording
- How can teachers record progress as well as achievement?

Reporting
- How can schools make reporting to parents part of a continuing dialogue between home and school?

CHAPTER 5

The Learning Environment

Rationale

With the current emphasis on matters such as National Curriculum attainment targets, programmes of study, assessment tasks and reporting to parents, it would be easy to dismiss spending time thinking about how the classroom is organised as a luxury teachers cannot afford. Many teachers would endorse the view that 'it would be very nice if only I had the time ...'. Whilst this view may be understandable initially, it is, we think, mistaken. It assumes that the way classrooms are set out, organised and managed is somehow separate from the more pressing and immediate tasks with which teachers are engaged. Teachers might regard classroom organisation and management as yet another item on an overcrowded list, or they can regard it as the bringing together of many of their ideas about teaching and learning. In fact the way classrooms are organised and managed is fundamental to achieving success in many of the areas we have explored in earlier chapters. The classroom will reflect a teacher's view about how children learn, and it will reflect a teacher's view of what it means to be a teacher. It is the place where curriculum planning is given the acid test, and the theories of continuous teacher assessment confront the everyday reality of a class of maybe 35 young children with widely differing needs.

It is vital that the way in which classrooms are set up, organised and managed is the result of some careful thought and consideration. It should be central to a teacher's curriculum planning and his or her role as the teacher. We would emphasise here that we are not simply discussing how we can make a classroom attractive (although that may be important), but how to create an environment which is specifically designed as a place where a teacher's ideas about teaching and learning will bear fruit. In that sense, how the classroom is set up will demonstrate a teacher's experiences, values and attitudes. The classroom is able to open or close opportunities for children, it will give them messages about a teacher's expectations, and will indicate to them explicitly and implicitly how they should conduct themselves. It is not hard to think of some common examples. If art materials are left dirty and untidy in a corner of the room, what message is that giving? A book area full of tatty books, poorly displayed, with a threadbare piece of carpet covering the floor is conveying attitudes and values about reading and books. If the teacher's attention must be attracted every time a pupil needs a piece of equipment, what does that say about opportunities for children to make their own decisions? The examples are endless, but the idea is simple – a classroom says a great deal about the teacher, to colleagues, to children, and increasingly to parents. A teacher's classroom is becoming an open arena, as the public face of the education system, and that is a major reason for ensuring it is the result of careful planning.

In the course of such planning there are a number of considerations that it is important to bear in mind. In purely pragmatic terms, no-one wants to spend the majority of the working day in a dreary, dull and dirty classroom, which reflects an air of neglect and disregard. Teachers and children will respond to rooms that are attractive, clean and ordered. Classrooms are not passive environments in which teaching and learning happens to take place – they should be designed to promote and enhance learning. They should motivate and stimulate, and they should be planned to make the most efficient use of the most important resource – namely the teacher. Earlier chapters will have indicated the range of possible activities teachers may be engaged in and classroom organisation should support teachers in their efforts to make them more efficient in using their time effectively. Later in this chapter we will explore the use of time in greater detail, but suffice it to say here that a guiding consideration of any form of classroom organisation must be to maximise a teacher's capacity to teach.

In the past thirty years architects and designers have spent a great deal of time in making sure new school buildings respond to the needs of pupils and teachers, and the most effective buildings are those which demonstrate collaboration between architects and teachers. Perhaps the lesson for teachers is that they too should design classrooms in a spirit of collaboration with the people who will work in them – in this case the children themselves. There is no one way to organise and run classrooms. All we are saying is that the way they are set up and managed should be just as much a part of a teacher's pedagogy as curriculum planning, teaching strategies or assessing learning.

Classroom Layout

When thinking about how classrooms are organised and managed most teachers will begin by considering how the furniture is laid out. As we have already emphasised this is a much more complex process than simply fitting all the furniture in, and making sure that everyone has a seat. A classroom layout should reflect a teacher's ideas about teaching and learning.

Depending on their approach to teaching and learning, teachers have broadly three options in terms of layout. The first of these options is to create a series of working areas within the classroom. These could include a reading area, a writing area, science area and maths area and possibly others depending on the age of the children. Within these working areas children would have easy access to an appropriate range of resources and materials. There are some clear advantages to this type of layout. It is easy for children to understand, and by providing a specific area designated for a particular activity pupils can be motivated and develop a sense of purpose. Resources and materials can be carefully matched to learning experiences, and will introduce children to the idea of specific resources relating to specific activities. This kind of layout however, has some drawbacks. Very few teachers will have enough space to create a sufficient number of areas that will represent the full range of activities they would wish to offer. The availability of resources can be limited to the group of children working within a particular area, and it can operate against making links across the curriculum. This kind of layout may be most appropriate for teachers who have a range of different activities going on at the same time. Typically a group of children could be engaged in a science experiment, others could be working on a maths investigation, whilst another group could be working with some construction material and so on, with anything up to five or six different activities. It is worth bearing in mind, however, some of the inherent difficulties associated with managing this number of activities (see Chapter 2).

The second and third options concerning classroom layout have a different focus. Rather than limiting resources to specific areas they look to organising the classroom in a more holistic way. In some respects these two options are more simple than the first (but not necessarily less effective!). Essentially the choice is between putting the resources and materials around the outside of the room, with children working in the middle, or putting the resources in the middle and children round the edges. The former is the more predominant pattern, but has the disadvantage of creating potentially more move-ment around the room. In the latter option, the theory is that all children have equal access to resourcing.

If we consider all three of these options, the reality is that many teachers opt for a mixture. Most classrooms have some designated areas, most commonly for wet or practical work, and a reading area. Other resources are usually stored around the edges of the room.

In virtually all primary school classrooms, space is at a premium. To make the most effective use of the available space, there are factors other than furniture layout to take into account. It is clearly the case that all children need space to work, but it may be less clear whether all children need their own place. The ways in which teachers wish to operate will have a bearing on how pupils are arranged.

The teacher who, when talking at length to the whole class, prefers children sat together in a carpeted area, and then disperses the child-ren to a variety of areas, with a variety of working partners, may not see the necessity for every child to have his or her own place. If one group will always be working on an activity that does not require desks or table space, then there is no need to have a place for every pupil. When space is limited this could be an important factor. When children are older, and sitting on the floor is less comfortable, or when there are an increasing number of occasions when everybody needs some desk or table space, then clearly this must be provided. The important message is to maintain a degree of flexibility. Modern furniture enables most teachers to provide a range of options. Putting tables together can save space, and enable a group of six or eight children to work together. Similarly the same tables arranged differ-ently can provide space for individual or paired work.

For different reasons many teachers are beginning to question whether they need a teacher's desk. The large desk which years ago invariably dominated classrooms no longer seems appropriate, and doing without it can save space. In the end it will be a question of teaching style. It would not be difficult for a teacher to monitor how often he or she sits at the desk, then to ask whether it is necessary to be sat at a desk and then to form some decisions. Those teachers who choose to keep a desk, should think carefully about where to place it. Should it be part of the working environment? Should it form a barrier between teachers and children, or should it be tucked away discreetly in a corner?

The lack of space is often most apparent when people are moving around the classroom. Most teachers will have experienced the exasperation of trying to reach over to a pupil, having to ask other pupils to 'just move over a bit'. It is equally frustrating for children when they are forced to squeeze past other children to collect equipment, or to get from one side of the room to the other. All this is very familiar, and in some classrooms some of this may be unavoidable. The sad fact is that there are still some classrooms that are too small for the number of pupils, but it is also a fact that some careful thought can begin to alleviate some problems. Planning a classroom layout is rather like creating a painting – sometimes it's the spaces left behind that are important. Organising routes around the classroom is important. Children need to be able to get from one part of the room to another, and this access should be planned. Observation will help in showing where congestion points occur. Resources that are in regular or constant demand could be placed strategically around the room rather than in one place. It is rarely the case that a teacher needs to be able to walk around four sides of a desk, or a group of tables. Space can be saved by grouping furniture together and by careful positioning around the room.

As previously indicated the main factor when planning a classroom is to keep a degree of flexibility. It should not be thought of as a once a year activity but should be something that is open to development and evolution through trial and error. Often classrooms carefully planned and arranged during the holidays look very different when the children actually take over. Many teachers are increasingly involving pupils in planning the layout and design of their room. This can be very effective and beneficial and will often provide some startling insights into how pupils actually see things. Even the youngest children can be involved in making decisions about where things are put, and how the tables are arranged. The ways in which children experience the classroom will be very different from the ways in which the teacher does. The wise teacher will tap into that experience and involve them in making some decisions. It is also perhaps worth remembering that redesigning the layout can motivate and stimulate both teacher and children.

Before leaving the discussion about classroom layout and design it is worth thinking carefully about the relationship between the layout and atmosphere. A room with predominantly hard straight edges, with desks laid out in a square or rectangular pattern, will have a very different feel from one arranged in curves, where the routes are more meandering. Many things will contribute to classroom atmosphere, but layout is certainly a factor. Carpets, plants and fabrics are great civilising influences as well as having many practical uses.

Designing a classroom is an important task. It is not only a case of fitting everyone in: it should express the teacher's views about learning and make a significant impact upon how teachers and children work together.

Resourcing

Providing an appropriate range of books and materials for children's use has always been an issue in primary schools. It is one that has become more acute with the onset of National Curriculum and the need to provide a range of equipment for subjects such as science and technology, as well as up-to-date and accessible books to support the development of reading skills.

The injection of additional funding for the resourcing of some National Curriculum subjects, and the five year Department of Education and Science scheme (now the Department for Education) for matched funding for information technology, has undoubtedly increased schools' capitation budgets, although the extra finance has not always been directed at those areas where there was greatest need at individual school level! The need to manage resources effectively, as well as the importance of planning for development in the long term, has led in many schools to the development of a whole school resourcing policy. This will guide decisions about priority areas for funding in each financial year, as well as indicating where resources can be centralised for use throughout a school, and what should form basic classroom equipment.

Class teachers may be guided (or constrained) by such policies when thinking about equipping their classrooms, or they may inherit a classroom which is already provided with a range of books and materials. Whatever the situation in which they find themselves, teachers will want to ensure that, as far as possible, their own classrooms are appropriately resourced to support children's learning.

The following are key issues for consideration by every teacher when thinking about the organisation of resources in the classroom.

Quality. This is a far more important element than quantity. Teachers are natural hoarders, and loathe to discard items which may have outlived their usefulness, but there is little point in shelf space being taken up by outdated or tatty books (which children will avoid using) or cupboards being full of games or jigsaws with pieces missing. The quality of the resources will affect the quality of the learning.

Appropriateness. Is there a variety of equipment suitable for the planned curriculum, and for the range of abilities within the class? If the school has a policy on centralised resources it may be important to think in terms of a basic equipment list for each classroom and planning activities which will make use of centralised resources at specific times.

Storage. Resources and materials should be appropriately stored so that a system is evident to the children. Resource areas (not necessarily work areas) can be established, so that all the equipment for a particular subject is collected in a clearly defined location. Colour coding for drawers, and storage boxes with pictorial labels for younger children can help with efficient use of equipment by pupils.

Accessibility. The more that children can organise resources for themselves the less time should be spent by a teacher on low-level tasks such as giving out paper. Children need to be clear about what they have immediate access to, and what can only be used with permission or under supervision. However, the vast majority of materials in a classroom should be available for children to select for appropriate use.

Consideration should be given to providing basic equipment for continual use such as pots of pencils, a variety of types of paper, and to organising other materials for ease of access. In order to do this in some classrooms, it may be necessary to remove cupboard doors to provide open shelving, or to purchase some inexpensive and colourful storage such as stackerjacks or plastic baskets.

If children are to make good use of the facilities available in a classroom they need to be clear about the system which operates. They may need to be trained in making appropriate use of resources, and in selecting materials for a particular task. They can play a role in managing classroom resources, and it may be useful to involve them in preliminary planning when organising the equipment for a particular curriculum area. Sometimes, if the system is not working effectively, they can have some useful observations to make on why things go wrong!

Giving children responsibility for ensuring that the resource system works well is an important aspect of developing independence from the teacher. They should be able, or if young be trained, in the collection, use, return and replacement of materials with minimal reference to the teacher. Where equipment is limited, they can be encouraged to negotiate with other children over the use of a particular resource. Negotiation and sharing equipment are important elements in planning tasks.

Responsibility for the overall management of resources is part of the teacher's role. A regular review of the use of equipment and materials is necessary to ensure that the system is working well, and that children's needs are being met. A regular audit, probably on an annual basis, should highlight shortages of materials, broken or inappropriate equipment, and anything in need of replenishment, replacement, or discarding.

As part of managing classroom resources, the teacher should consider some flexibility in provision. Whilst there should be a wide variety of materials and appropriate equipment to provide for a range of activities, not all equipment needs to be available at all times. Available facilities should link with curriculum planning, both long and short term, and there is a need to consider some freshness of appeal in introducing new equipment or limiting availability. The overall school policy may, of course, influence provision at times.

Using Extra Help

The last twenty years have seen a dramatic shift in perceptions in terms of additional adults working alongside teachers in classrooms. In the early 1970s, ancillary assistants in primary schools were used as extra office staff, often controlling the ordering and provision of stock, as first aiders, and as recorders of a wide range of television and radio programmes. Their role in classrooms was generally limited because they had a number of commitments throughout the school. Parents occasionally helped in schools, generally with tasks outside classrooms such as covering books and mounting pupils' work for display. The classroom was very much the province of the teacher, whose role was quite distinct from that of parents and non-teaching staff.

The spread of a number of initiatives in the 1980s, which were designed to encourage home – school partnerships, led to a recognition in primary schools of the potential for parents to support their own children's learning, as well as having a role to play in helping with a range of activities in classrooms.

Most schools have also had a considerable increase in the time, and now funding, allocated for ancillary assistants. This factor, coupled with a shift in thinking about the importance of providing additional adult help wherever possible in classrooms, has led to many teachers having extra adult assistance during some part of the week.

Whilst the teacher still has the key responsibility as the children's educator, extra adults in classrooms can play a complementary role in supporting children's learning. Additional help may be provided by a number of different groups. Ancillary assistants and parents have already been mentioned but in addition there may be governors, pupils from a local secondary school on work experience, students training for a career in health, social work or education and various other interested parties! Help may be provided on a regular basis for a short time every week, or it may be available every day for a concentrated period. Whatever the situation, most teachers at some time will find themselves needing to think about the effective use of an extra adult in the classroom.

Managing the work of other adults, and, in particular, working in partnership with parents, is an area in which few teachers have received guidance. The work of Atkin and Bastiani (1988) on training to work with parents concluded that much needed to be done 'both in initial training and in in-service training'. Research conducted by Jowett and colleagues on behalf of the National Foundation of Education Research (1991) on parental involvement in schools, found that about half the teachers involved in the study felt that some sort of training on working with parents was necessary.

Making the best use of additional help is a challenging task, and there are a number of factors to consider. Some schools have an agreed policy on helpers in the classroom, although often these refer exclusively to parent helpers. This type of policy may cover such matters as the deployment of helpers, the organisation of rotas for assistance in various classes, and the types of tasks which helpers might be asked to undertake. Such a policy should also be very clear about the sensitivities involved in parents working in schools, and it is important to point out to parents that the behaviour and abilities of the children should not be the subject of discussion outside the classroom. Where such policies exist, there will obviously be some initial guidance for teachers, and some decisions made for them about making use of extra help. However, individual teachers still have a responsibility for organising the work of helpers and for supporting them in the classroom. Time taken for careful planning of this aspect of classroom management, and the development of a system for effective guidance for helpers, is time well invested in making good use of a very valuable asset.

Schools, and perhaps individual teachers, will have different systems for organising the deployment of helpers. Some assistance, particularly from ancillary staff, may be timetabled, whilst volunteer help will probably be negotiated. Before issuing a request for helpers, it is worth spending time to consider the following questions:

- Do I want extra help at any time or on specific occasions?
- Are there activities with which extra help would be particularly valuable?

When people volunteer their services, or are allocated to the classroom, some time needs to be invested in negotiating how they are going to work. It is important to discover whether helpers have particular interests or areas of expertise to offer, and whether there are certain activities with which they would prefer not to become involved. Time taken for this sort of discussion transmits important messages to helpers about the value a teacher places on their services.

Helpers also need the opportunity to develop some understanding about such matters as classroom routine, expectations of the children in terms of behaviour and ways of working, and the system for organisation of activities and resources. Much of this understanding will take time to develop, but some potential difficulties can be prevented if a teacher can be quite explicit at the outset about the way the classroom functions, and how the children are expected to work.

When a helper arrives in a classroom, he or she needs clear direction if the time being given is going to be of use. It is important to have one particular task on which to focus, with clear instructions on how to organise the activity. Brief written guidance which highlights the main aims of the task can assist a helper in clearly understanding its purpose. There should also be an opportunity for some discussion when the activity is completed, for this demonstrates the value that the teacher has placed on the extra help, as well as providing information on how the helper has coped and what the children have achieved. The initial written guidance can help to focus the discussion on any particular areas where the teacher would find information useful.

The status of helpers is dependent upon the time a teacher takes to plan their activities, and the types of tasks in which they become involved. The deployment of adult helpers carries implicit messages. If a helper, rather than the teacher, is always involved in one particular activity such as art, what does that say to pupils about the status of art in the curriculum? If a helper hears children read, does he or she work in the same surroundings and operate in the same way as the teacher or, for instance, be based outside the classroom ? Answers to these questions will also indicate messages about the importance of different adults in the classrooms.

As well as developing strategies for making effective use of extra help, consideration also needs to be given to the perceptions of adults, usually parents, who cannot be involved in the classroom. The NFER research highlighted the views of a substantial number of parents who would have liked to see fewer parents helping in schools. Their comments showed a lack of understanding of the role and value of helpers as complementary to the teacher, rather than as a substitute. Schools or individual teachers obviously need to be quite explicit about the role of classroom helpers and convey appropriate information through the school prospectus, newsletters and written invitations to come and help, as well as through discussions with governors, parents' associations and with individuals.

Display

The issue of display in primary classrooms is something that regularly exercises the minds of all class teachers. It is a problem that by and large is peculiar to primary schools, although increasingly secondary schools are eager to present an attractive image and now regularly display pupil work in the public areas. The fact that some teachers see display as simply a means of making classrooms more attractive creates some problems. If the reason for creating attractive displays were only a cosmetic activity, then teachers could legitimately question how such an activity claims any priority on their time.

Whilst it is a reasonable intention to make classrooms more attractive, if that were the sole reason for advocating display then it would not be worthy of much attention. The business of display is much more than brightening up dull corners, covering cracks, and double mounting: it is another important factor in ensuring classrooms are places in which effective learning can take place. Display has three distinct uses: it can celebrate, stimulate and inform. How display is used to promote these three functions will also transmit values and messages to children, parents and colleagues. For example, what you choose to celebrate will begin to give messages about what is valued or who is held in high esteem. How you begin to stimulate and inform through display will illustrate some clear ideas about how you regard children and their learning. The transmission of values and attitudes is a dimension that touches all aspects of display, but it is worthwhile thinking about each of the three ways display can be used. What will also become clear is that the distinctions we have proposed are quite arbitrary, since in many cases there will be considerable overlap.

Enjoying and acknowledging children's achievement is an important aspect of any classroom. Displaying those achievements is just one way of demonstrating the regard in which their work is held, but there are many others. One of the restrictions of displaying pupils' work has been that it has led to an over emphasis on the product or outcome, at the expense of the process. It is not too difficult to redress this imbalance. If we consider for a moment the way modern libraries and museums have been eager not only to display authors' and artists' finished items, but to acquire the notebooks, jottings, sketch pads and rough drawings to demonstrate the development of the works, we can perhaps begin to see how schools can also start to acknowledge the process. As teachers who are concerned with process and outcome, it is important that we place equal value on each. Efforts at drafting can be displayed alongside the finished stories, sketches and jottings shown next to the completed art work. This gives clear messages, not least that behind good outcomes, there is usually a great deal of hard work, and that hard work is worth acknowledging and displaying.

There are other, perhaps more fundamental, considerations about displaying work. As part of Andrew Pollard's 'social policy for the classroom' (see Chapter 2), display is one way of promoting children's self-image, and giving them a sense of worth. The converse is also true. Failing to display some pupils' work may go some way to alienating those children from the classroom. This is an area where teachers must use their judgement. It is important that all children have work displayed (not all at the same time!) but it is equally important that such work is worthy of display, and is of some significance. Display can also demonstrate the achievements of groups of pupils working towards a common end, as well as the achievements of individuals. Indeed, presenting work in different forms as individuals, and as a member of a group, is part of National Curriculum requirements.

The most effective displays of children's work pay some regard to basic aesthetic considerations. The most attractive displays are the result of some thought concerning shape, colour, form and texture. This not only boosts children's confidence in seeing their work promoted in this way, but, perhaps more importantly, it provides an opportunity to discuss these features, as well as some guidance for children when they begin to set up their own displays.

What is displayed in classrooms can form part of the learning process. A good dramatic, thought-provoking display can provide great stimulation for learning. There are countless ways in which children can be motivated by something they can see, observe, smell, touch or hear. Science investigations can start with a display which challenges through effective questioning, and promotes the development of skills, for example, 'use the magnifying glass to observe, record what you see ...', 'what do you think will happen if ...?', all of which can begin to make children think, discuss, predict and hypothesise. Similarly, display can stimulate an aesthetic or artistic response through careful use of colours, textures, and forms. In the humanities, a collection of artefacts can be the starting point for enquiry and investigation. The most effective displays are often those which not only stimulate and motivate, but also show the results. As we noted earlier these uses of display to celebrate, stimulate and inform are not mutually exclusive and they will often be interlinked.

Inevitably, those displays which are concerned to motivate are also implicitly contributing to the third aspect of display, that of informing. The notion that display within the classroom can support young children's learning is the aspect that is least recognised. Stimulation and motivation are starting points for learning, but display can provide support once children have embarked upon their work. What is actually stuck up on the walls, or stood in a corner, or displayed on a table can act as a resource for the learner. This will vary from classroom to classroom, but it could include such items as current word lists, key phrases to reinforce an ongoing activity, the display of resource material alongside guidance on how to use it, or simple instructions about what to do in particular circumstances. The possibility of displaying the process alongside the outcomes can provide a source of support for other pupils and a focus for discussion.

Display has had a high profile in primary education, and as we discussed earlier, is often regarded, sometimes erroneously, as an indicator of effective learning. It is important that teachers think carefully about this, in the same way as they would think about any other classroom activity. Display makes a very significant contribution to the classroom climate. It is by its very nature a public statement which is there for children, colleagues and parents to see. As it is a significant factor in creating classroom atmosphere it is vital that we do not fall into the trap of 'surface rather than substance' (Alexander 1992), and that requires thought and consideration about how good display contributes to effective learning rather than simply making the room look nice.

The Use of Time

'All my possessions for a moment of time'. The final words of Elizabeth I will strike many chords in the minds of primary school teachers, who are frequently concerned with trying to squeeze too much activity into too little time. Recent legislation has appeared to exacerbate the already over-burdened task of teaching, but teachers have shown themselves remarkably effective in achieving a great deal in a short period. The introduction of the National Curriculum and accompanying assessment and reporting procedures have meant for many teachers a reappraisal of how they can make the best use of their time, and, just as importantly, it has encouraged all of us to ask how pupils should spend their time.

It is a truism that time is an important resource in any classroom, so it is vital that some clear thought is given as to how teachers and pupils actually use it. As we have already noted, studies of how children spend their time within the curriculum have shown a considerable degree of consistency. The most recent research (Alexander 1992) confirms earlier studies in which language accounts for around 30% of pupil time, and mathematics about 20%. Before the National Curriculum, science accounted for about 8.5%, but since its elevation to a core subject this figure has risen. All other areas of the curriculum receive significantly less time. Like all statistics, these figures hide a multitude of variations and can be misleading, but in the same study Alexander also noted that language and mathematics were the areas in which children spent the highest proportion of time distracted from their task. In other words there may be a danger of greater quantity leading to less quality. Looking at the time spent on different areas of the curriculum is useful in any consideration of curriculum balance, but it is not the only aspect worthy of study. The ten generic activities identified by Alexander – writing, apparatus, reading, listening/looking, drawing/painting, collaboration, movement, talking to teacher, construction, talking to class – perhaps represent a view of the curriculum which is much closer to the experience of young children than that laid down in statutory orders. When planning a range of activities which provide a balanced set of learning opportunities it is important to consider these ten activities as well as the National Curriculum subjects. Within these ten activities, writing and reading take up a large percentage of time. It would be unwise to draw too many conclusions from these statistics, but it would be foolish to ignore some of the issues which they raise.

It would be useful to ask ourselves some questions when thinking about planning pupil and teacher time.

- If the largest proportion of time spent off-task by pupils occurs in those curriculum areas to which most time is devoted (and the converse is true), what are the implications for the amount of time spent on different curriculum areas?
- If we monitor the generic activities that pupils are engaged in, rather than curriculum areas, can we begin to provide a genuinely balanced range of experiences over a period of time?

To a large degree these are questions of planning rather than classroom management and organisation. But they do impinge upon classroom practice. Careful observation and pupil tracking would begin to give some idea about what kind of diet individual pupils were being offered. Asking pupils to review their activities, concentrating upon what they actually did rather than the subjects studied, could be helpful. A check-list of generic activities could be provided to help pupils in doing this, and could also be used by a teacher when reviewing curriculum plans.

Once time has figured in planning, how can we begin to make sure that the plans bear fruit in the classroom, and ensure it is spent in the most effective way by both pupils and teachers? The best way to begin is to explore the ways in which time is currently used. How much time is spent in various non-curricular activities such as coming into the room, settling down, registration, and so on? What does a typical teaching session look like in terms of time? Alexander's study timed various 'teaching' sessions and broke them down into sections, demonstrating that the amount of time spent on teaching and learning, as opposed to routine matters, differed considerably from classroom to classroom. The details are in Chapter 2 (see Table 2.1, page 37), but the conclusions illustrated that on average children spent:

59% of time working
11% in routine activities
8% waiting for the teacher or adult
21% being distracted
1% other (unclassified)

It was these figures which led to newspaper headlines proclaiming that primary pupils spent 40% of their time not working. The study distanced itself from the popular rhetoric, but nevertheless, the figures represent averages which mean that in some classrooms it must be the case that pupils must spend over 40% of time not working. No one is suggesting that pupils should work 100% of the time, but there is clearly something amiss when such an amount of time appears lost.

It would be most appropriate for teachers to use the evidence from their own classrooms as the basis for developing strategies which maximise pupils' learning opportunities. Without being too specific, there are some key factors that teachers could take into account. The establishment of clearly understood routines could minimise time-wasting. These routines would affect the start and finish of teaching sessions, would ensure that tidying-up was efficient and quick, and messages would be given about teacher expectations if pupils knew that when they come into the room certain activities should be under-taken. There may well be an element of training to introduce children to these routines, but that could be seen as a good investment in time-saving. Routines can also be appropriate in working arrangements, and support strategies for learning can be clearly outlined. For example, what does a pupil do if needing help with spelling? Is there a procedure for this which is clearly understood? If a pupil has finished what should he or she do? Investing effort in solving those problems that eat away at a teacher's time will be important in making sure time is well spent.

Managing and planning the use of time should not be seen as providing a rigid framework. A well-managed classroom will also have a degree of flexibility to allow for the unexpected, and also to allow pupils to engage in some periods of sustained work. One factor in ensuring quality of learning, as well as quality of outcome, is having sufficient time for the task in hand.

Perhaps the most important factor in considering the use of time are the questions about what the teacher actually does. There is some evidence (ORACLE 1980, Mortimore et al 1988) that teachers are not always the best judges as to what they actually do, and there is some-times a difference between rhetoric and practice. There is an increas-ingly powerful body of research (Mortimore et al 1988, Tharp and Gallimore 1988) which indicates some of the characteristics of teaching which are judged to be effective. As we begin to learn more about these strategies, it would seem appropriate that teachers should be managing their time in such a way as to maximise the opportuni-ties to put these into effect. These strategies include questioning, instructing, and giving critical feedback. Each of these strategies has been explored in some depth earlier in the book, but it is worth emphasising that when planning what the teacher does, time should be allocated to ensure that these key teaching strategies do occur, and that routine, low-level servicing activities in which some teachers get bogged down be kept to a minimum. Time is such an important commodity that its use cannot be left to chance. All the same, more does not necessarily mean better. The management of time is only one part of the total equation in making teaching more effective and learning more productive.

This chapter has suggested many ways in which teachers can begin to organise and manage their classrooms to maximise opportunities for effective learning. The 'Starting Points' below form an agenda through which teachers can begin to review their own practice. Whilst it is important for individual teachers to reflect on their own work, many teachers are finding it helpful to work in collaboration with colleagues through activities such as paired observation and self-evaluation. We think that the suggestions and ideas included in this chapter would form a sound basis for those kinds of activities.

Starting Points

Rationale
- What messages does your classroom convey about you as a teacher?
- What messages does your classroom convey to pupils about your expectations of them?
- How does your classroom promote and support learning?

Classroom Layout
- Does the furniture layout allow opportunities for class, group and individual work?
- Are there clear routes and pathways around the classroom?
- How have the pupils been involved in making decisions about the layout?

Resourcing
- When was the last time a resource audit was carried out?
- Are resources organised systematically and accessible to all children?
- How do you judge the appropriateness and quality of your resources?

Using Extra Help
- What kind of support and guidance do you offer helpers in your classroom?

- How do you make helpers feel valued?
- How do you make sure that helpers get involved in a variety of tasks?

Display
- Do the displays in your room serve a variety of purposes?
- What opportunities do you provide for all pupils to contribute to displays?
- How do your displays demonstrate the process behind the outcomes?

The Use of Time
- How do you monitor the use of your time?
- How do you maximise the time children are actively engaged in learning activities?
- Are there a variety of routines clearly understood by children which cut down on time-wasting?

Bibliography

Alexander, R. (1992) *Policy and Practice in Primary Education* (London and New York: Routledge).

Alexander, R., Rose, J. and Woodhead, C. (1992) *Curriculum Organisation and Classroom Practice in Primary Schools* (London: Department of Education and Science).

Athey, C. (1990) *Extending Thought in Young Children: a Parent-Teacher Partnership* (London: Paul Chapman).

Atkin, J. and Bastiani, J. with Goode, J. (1988) *Listening to Parents* (London, New York, Sydney: Croom Helm).

Bassey, M. (1986) 'Does action research require sophisticated research methods?' in *Action Research in Classrooms and Schools,* Hussler, D. et al (London: Allen and Unwin).

Bennett, N. (1987) 'Changing Perspectives on Teaching Learning Processes', *Oxford Review of Education,* **13**(1).

Bennett, N. (1992) Managing Learning in Primary Classrooms in the *Managing Primary Education Series* (Stoke-on-Trent: ASPE/Trentham Books).

Bennett, N. and Dunne, E. (1992) *Managing Classroom Groups* (Hemel Hempstead: Simon and Schuster).

Bennett, N., Deforges, C., Cockburn, A. and Wilkinson, B. (1984) *The quality of pupil learning experiences* (Hove: Lawrence Erlbaum).

Bruner, J. (1986) *Actual Minds Possible Worlds* (Cambridge, Massachusetts and London: Harvard University Press).

Campbell, J. (1992) Managing Teachers' Time in Primary Schools: Concepts, Evidence and Policy Issues in the *Managing Primary Education Series* (Stoke-on-Trent: ASPE/Trentham Books).

Carr, W. and Kemmis, S. (1986) *Becoming Critical* (London: Falmer Press).

Cashdan, A. (1980) 'Teaching Language and Reading in the Early Years' in *The Reading Connection,* eds. Bray, G. and Hugh, A.G. (London: Ward Lock).

Cohen, E.G. (1986) *Designing Groupwork: Strategies for the Heterogeneous Classroom* (NewYork: Teachers College Press).

David, T., Curtis, A. and Siraj-Blatchford, I. (1993) *Effective teaching in the Early Years: fostering children's learning in nurseries and infant classrooms* (University of Warwick: Organisation Mondiale pour L'Education Prescolaire – U.K.).

Dearing, R. (1994) The National Curriculum and its Assessment: Final Report (London: School Curriculum and Assessment Authority).

Department for Education (1990) Management of the School Day (Circular 7/90).

Department of Education and Science (1967) *Children and their Primary Schools* (London: HMSO).

Dewey, J. (1933) *How we think: A Restatement of the Relation of Reflective Thinking in the Educational Process* (Chicago: Henry Regnery).

Donaldson, M. (1978) *Children's Minds* (Glasgow: Fontana).

Edwards, D. and Mercer, N. (1987) *Common Knowledge – The Development of Understanding in the Classroom* (London and New York: Routledge).

Fountain, S. (1990) Learning Together: Global Education 4–7 (Cheltenham: Stanley Thornes).

Galton, M. and Williamson, J. (1992) *Group Work in the Primary Classroom* (London and New York: Routledge).

Galton, M., Simon, B. and Croll, P. (1980) *Inside the Primary Classroom* (London: Routledge and Kegan Paul).

Gelman, R. (1969) 'Conservation Acquisition: A problem of learning to attend to relevant attributes', *Journal of Experimental Child Psychology,* **7**, 167–198.

Gipps, C. (1992) What we Know about Effective Primary Teaching from the series The London File – Papers from the Institute of Education (London: Tufnell Press).

Golby, M. (1993) *Reflective Professional Practice: A Reader* (Tiverton: Fair Way Publications).

Hughes, M., Wikeley, F. and Nash, T. (1990) Parents and the National Curriculum, An Interim Report (Exeter: School of Education).

Jackson, M. (1987) 'Making sense of school' in *Children and their Primary Schools,* ed. Pollard, A. (Lewes: Falmer Press).

Jowett, S. and Baginsky, M. with MacDonald MacNeil, M. (1991) *Building Bridges – parental involvement in schools* (Windsor: NFER–Nelson).

MacGilchrist, B. (1992) Managing Access and Entitlement in Primary Education in the *Managing Primary Education Series* (Stoke-on-Trent: ASPE/Trentham Books).

McAuley, H. and Jackson, P. (1992) *Educating Young Children: A Structural Approach* (London: David Fulton).

Meadows, S. and Cashdan, A. (1988) *Helping Children Learn*

(London: David Fulton).

Moll, L.C. (1990) *Vygotsky and Education* (Cambridge: Cambridge University Press).

Mortimore, P., Sammons, P., Stoll, L., Lewis, D. and Ecob, R. (1988) *School Matters* (Wells: Open Books).

Moyles, J. (1992) *Organizing for Learning in the Primary Classroom* (Buckingham and Philadelphia: Open University Press).

Norman, K. ed. (1992) *Thinking Voices: Work of the National Oracy Project* (London, Sydney and Auckland: Hodder and Stoughton).

Office for Standards in Education (1993) Classroom Organisation and Classroom Practice in Primary Schools (London: Ofsted).

Pollard, A. (1985) *The Social World of the Primary School* (London, New York, Sydney and Toronto: Holt, Rinehart and Winston).

Pollard, A. ed. (1987) *Children and their Primary Schools* (London, New York and Philadelphia: Falmer Press).

Pollard, A. and Tann, S. (1987) *Reflective Teaching in the Primary School* (London: Cassell).

Rowland, S. (1984) *The Enquiring Classroom* (London and New York: Falmer Press).

Silveira, W.R. and Trafford, G. (1988) *Children need groups* (Aberdeen: Aberdeen University Press).

Tharp, R.G. and Gallimore, R. (1988) Rousing Minds to Life (Cambridge: Cambridge University Press).

Tizard, B., Blatchyard, P., Burke, J., Farquhar, C. and Plewis, I. (1988) *Young Children at School in the Inner City* (London: Lawrence Erlbaum Associates).

Topping, K. (1985) 'An introduction to paired reading' in *Parental Involvement in Children's Reading,* eds. Topping, K. and Wolfendale, S. (London: Croom Helm).

Vygotsky, L.S. (1962) *Thought and Language* (New York: Wiley).

Webb, N.M. (1989) 'Peer interaction and learning in small groups', *International Journal of Educational Research,* **13,** 21–39.

Wood, D. (1988) *How Children Think and Learn* (Oxford: Blackwell).

Wood, D. (1992) Teaching Talk: How modes of Teacher Talk affect Pupil Participation in *Thinking Voices,* ed. Norman, K. (London, Sydney and Auckland: Hodder and Stoughton).

Wragg, E., Bennett, N. and Carré, C. (1989) Primary Teachers and the National Curriculum: Research Paper in Education, **4**(3).

Zeichner, K.M. and Liston, P. (1987) 'Teaching Student Teachers to Reflect' *Harvard Educational Review,* **57**(1), 23–48.

Index